FINDING GOD'S LOVE

The Theory and Practice of Love and Devotion as a Spiritual Path

Ethan Walker III

Devi Press
PO Box 5081, Norman, OK 73070
www.devipress.com

Published by:

Devi Press, Inc.
PO Box 5081
Norman, OK 73070
405-447-0364
www.devipress.com

Library of Congress Control Number, 2003103581

Printed in the United States of America
Oklahoma City, Oklahoma
ISBN # 0-9729317-1-6

Contact the author: ethan@devipress.com

And what is wisdom?

Wisdom is knowing we are all one.
Love is what it feels like
And compassion is what it acts like.

God is Love

1 John 4:8

ACKNOWLEDGMENTS

The author wishes to express his deep gratitude
to his teacher and mentor the Holy Mother, Ammachi,
without whose grace this book could not have been written.

Also thank you to Swami Amritaswarupananda
for permission to reprint the large volume of Amma's quotes that
were originally penned by him.

Thank you to my wife Marsha
for her support, encouragement, and invaluable editing.

Thank you to all my spiritual brothers and sisters
who make the writing of this book meaningful.

Other books by the author include:

The Mystic Christ:
The light of non-duality and the path of love according
to the life and teaching of Jesus

Soft Moon Shining:
Poems for the Mother of the universe

A brief description of these books can be found in the back of this book.
They may be thoroughly explored and purchased on-line at
www.devipress.com or call 405-447-0364 for a free brochure.

Contents

⟨ INTRODUCTION

Finding God's Love is a how-to book written for those of us who are
interested in exploring the practice of love and devotion as a spiritual
path. This path is well articulated in Hindu and Buddhist scriptures
such as the *Bhakti Sutras* by Narada. The path of love was also cham-
pioned by Jesus, whose primary two commandments are to love God
with all our heart and love our neighbor as our own self. In both of
the Master's commandments, love is the operative principle.

This book is suitable for all persons and all faiths. Devotional practice can be extended to one's chosen form of God, whether that be
Allah, Buddha, God the Father, God the Mother, Tara, Krishna,
Shiva, Isis, Jehovah, Great Spirit, Kwan Yin, Elohim, Mother Mary,
Jesus, or one's own satguru. The reader should feel free to substitute
one's own chosen form of God while learning to apply the practices
and principals in this work.

The first part of this book was written by the author in an attempt to
present the many benefits regarding the path of love and devotion.
It contains both theory and practice and will hopefully provide the
reader with some background for reading the latter part of the book,
titled *Instruction from Ammachi*. This is a collection of Amma's
own words. She directs the soul to embrace God and all the beings
in the universe in the fiery heart of love and thereby find liberation
from mortality and suffering. The author regards his own words to
be merely a preparatory introduction to the radiant diamond-clear
instructions from Amma that form the centerpiece of this book. Like
Jesus, Ammachi recommends the path of devotion and selfless love
as her primary teaching. She followed this same path to merge with
God and became permanently fixed in the Supreme while still a
teenager. Like a bird splashing in an open pool, the lover of God
will delight in the joyous presence and words of the Holy Mother.

Some introduction to Ammachi is necessary for those who have not
acquainted themselves with her. In October of 2002, Ammachi was
awarded the prestigious international Gandhi-King award. This
award is named after Mahatma Gandhi and Martin Luther King, Jr.
and is given each year to the person who has contributed the most to

non-violence in this world. Prior to that, she was one of a few delegates chosen to represent India at the Parliament of Religions held at the United Nations building. Ammachi believes that all of the world's major religions are paths to God. When she is asked about her own religion, she replies that it is love.

Ammachi was born in 1953 to a poor family of fisher folk in southern India. Her path is love, and her life is one of unending and unparalleled compassion. Ammachi spends ten or twelve hours of most days of the week hugging all comers, consoling them and blessing them with her divine love. To date, it is calculated that she has hugged over twenty million people. In India it is not uncommon for her to hug ten to twenty thousand in a single sitting. Can we imagine ourselves even lifting our arm to make the embrace ten or twenty thousand times in a single day? At the end of each hugging session, at four, five, or six o'clock in the morning, she will still be smiling, fresh, and taking just as much time with each person as she did when the first pilgrim arrived in her lap. Many people have reported miraculous healings and spiritual awakenings, but most importantly, they feel the unimaginably powerful love that pours out of her like a great, untamed river. She sacrifices the whole of her being everyday for the welfare of every soul. To find a person with this much love is extremely rare and fortuitous.

Amma is the author and instigator of numerous charitable activities, including an 800 bed state-of-the-art hospital, orphanages, housing for the destitute, feeding of the poor, pensions for widows, education, and much more.

She asks nothing but gives everything. No collection plate is passed. There is nothing to join. She does not ask that we reconstruct our beliefs or pledge allegiance to her or her organization. Members of any faith are welcome and encouraged to excel in their own chosen path. The Holy Mother will help them. Ammachi is pure, unconditional love incarnate. And what is love? God is love. By their fruits we will know them.

The reader is encouraged to examine the life of Ammachi as a study in the practice of devotion. Information for purchasing her biography is at the end of this book or visit her web site, www.ammachi.org.

CHAPTER 1

A Call to Love

Love is the eternal luminescence that radiates from the center of all beings and all existence. Love is the unifying presence of the One that still reverberates in this hall of mirrors we call "the many." Individual sparks, souls, beings, and universes without end appear to hurtle away from each other as though shot from the cannon of creation. Yet love remains the bond – the elastic stretching tether of infinity that ever belies the illusion of separation. Once discovered, love invites us backstage where "the many" is revealed to be a glorious sleight of hand.

The universe itself is an act of poetic love in which the Divine Mother, who is all form, expresses Her inconceivable affection and devotion for Her eternal lover, the pure formless Absolute. The Absolute, as the Divine Father, is the unchanging witness of the Divine Mother's dance. As pure infinite consciousness, He is bound by ecstatic love to be the Mother's eternal audience as She spins Her web of inconceivable beauty in the Grand Emptiness of time and space. Gripped in the fire of love, the Divine Pair play out the eons like two inseparable children embracing each other in love's endless bliss. Every atom, every star, every sentient being and countless universes without end are like waves perpetually arising from the ocean of love and perpetually disappearing back into it again.

Love is the one true wealth – the brilliant, shining diamond in the ebb and flow of existence. Love reveals the beauty in all things, or better said, love is revealed as the beauty in all things. Love is the cry of a child and its mother's warm embrace. Love is a human being absorbed in compassion and crying with deep tears at seeing the suffering of another. Love is one ocean wave after another caressing the sand and rocks; it is lightning dancing and thunder roaring and a bee in search of the most fragrant flower. God is revealed to those who love.

Only love can liberate us while yet binding us in the unity of our common being. Love is the glowing fire that grants meaning to our lives, freeing us from the prison of boredom and restlessness. Love extracts no payment. Expecting nothing, love is like an endless fountain bubbling up from the ground of being. Love gives freely to all Her children, saint and sinner alike. Love is the soothing antidote to the burning poison of self-centered delusion. Our own life is a sacred gift given to us in love by our Divine Mother and Father. Love is innocence and love is the fulfillment of all life.

Love is the true benefactor of any society. A loving people will naturally aspire to the vision of the Whole and thereby arrive at a sense of caring, a compassion for the Whole. With love as our light, we live harmoniously and effectively. This yields concentration of effort, which is the dynamo of any social order. A society whose people have become trapped in the delusion of a self-centered existence will reap the bitter fruit of fragmentation, chaos, and destruction.

Without love we are lost. Therefore, the practice of love is the most important aspect of our human existence and benefits society in a most practical way. May each of us be inspired to learn how to love and, in our newfound joy and cosmic exuberance, shout from the rooftops, "Love is all you need!"

Theory of the Path of Love

LOVE AS A SPIRITUAL PATH

Almost without exception, each of us has assumed some direction or path that we believe will deliver us into the open arms of happiness. The pursuit of happiness is our common human motivating force. The limitless number of paths to happiness that are available to us can be distilled into two categories: the outward path and the spiritual path. Each of us is consciously or unconsciously pursuing one or the other or some combination of the two.

THE OUTWARD PATH

The outward path is everything that appears to be outside of us; in other words, objects. An object is any item, be it person, place, or thing, that appears to any of the senses. It is anything that can be observed, including our own body. This is the path that most of us take in order to find happiness. It is really not a path to happiness, because it ultimately leads to disappointment, frustration, and depression. We have a deeply rooted belief that acquiring these objects will, in some way, make us happy. If we look more deeply into our own minds, however, we will see that acquiring these objects is a contrived, fool's gold happiness, and we will find them to be no more than temporary relief from our nagging desires. It is the expectation of relief from the tension of desire that makes these objects appear attractive, like an itching mosquito bite. The itching compels us to scratch, and this provides a momentary blissful relief. We are happy because the itch has stopped. Later, the itching returns and we are once again compelled to scratch. For example, we may experience elation in purchasing items. When we make purchases, we are temporarily elated and satisfied, but soon the feeling goes away, and we are compelled by our desires to chase after another round of intoxication. We pull our credit card from our billfold and reenact our campaign of consumerism. As with all such attempts to find happiness through objects, the purchases must ever escalate in order to scratch the itch. We are faced with a diminishing ratio of satisfaction to objects acquired. In other words, it takes more stuff to get high each time we scratch the itch.

In the following poem, the great Muslim poet Hafiz[1] comments on the illusion of happiness-in-objects, calling it a bag of magic tricks. Hafiz frequently uses wine as a metaphor for the intoxication of love for God, whom he refers to as the Winebringer.

MAGIC TRICKS

O Sufi, come and open this bag of tricks;
This is a trap. Release all this sorcery to the sky –

This is like the juggler who hides an egg in his armpit and
    then
Makes it disappear, and later finds it hidden in his cap.

Winebringer, more wine! The friend of the Sufis is here
And is giving gifts of great beauty and singing songs of
    grace.

O heart, come here, so we can go over to the house of God
And be far away from all these magic tricks.

Remember, it does not pay to play any games but the Game
    of Love;
He who makes his own heart disappear is only leaving the
    door open for trouble to get in.

---

[1] Hafiz was born in the fourteenth century as Khwaja Shamsuddin Muhammad in what is now known as Iraq.

When the truth is known, the magician and the juggler,
For all their tricks, will hide their heads in shame.

O you peacock who struts around proudly, where are you
    going?
Your pride is vulnerable to even a poor man's prayer.

Hafiz, don't be so hard on God's lovers and those who don't
    drink wine
Just because you are above hypocrisy and cheap tricks and
    haven't far to go.

Hafiz, *Drunk on the Wine of the Beloved - 100 Poems of Hafiz*, translated by Thomas Rain Crowe, Shambala Publications, Inc.

When asked, many of us will say with a smile that we are quite happy. What most of us mean is that we are happy to be striving for our objective goals such as a bigger house, luxury automobile, Mister or Miss Right, status, wealth, popularity, and power. As if in a hypnotic stupor, we are enchanted and mesmerized by the expectation of these things and not the reality of the present moment.

Wealth is a state of mind. A wealthy person is simply one who has everything he or she wants. This means it is possible to possess very little and be wealthy.

Conversely, there are many who have great wealth but are robbed of any personal peace or satisfaction by their insatiable desires. The whip of a deathlike emptiness drives them to acquire more. What most of us mean by "I am happy" is that we are happy to be working for our goals, imagining that we will someday possess the objects of our dreams – then we will, at last, be "truly happy." If these goals are not met, we suffer. If we meet these goals and then lose them, we suffer.

Unfortunately, the loss of the objects of our desires must surely come. If not now, then certainly when death knocks at our door. Like the weather and everything else in the universe, objects are part of the endlessly changing world of form. All objects are temporary. They come and they go like clouds in the summer sky. What we have today will certainly be gone at a future time. Our house, car, mother, father, spouse, money, will eventually evaporate like water on a hot rock, leaving us alone and bereft of any comfort that these things might have provided. We are encouraged by the rest of the world to pursue the fleeting and impermanent happiness of objects. Almost all of us are engaged in this chase of phantoms. We are like cattle, forced to walk down the narrow chute of our materialistic culture. Our parents, our teachers, movies, friends, books, and newspapers encourage us to take up the banner of happiness-through-objects from the time we are very young until the day we die. We are taught that happiness surely awaits those who steadfastly cling to the merry-go-round of producing, reproducing, and consuming. We *buy* in order to *be*. We abandon love in order to possess.

The Spiritual Path

> To have God in us is a struggle in the beginning, but if we persist, it will lead us to everlasting bliss and happiness. All struggles will end. To embrace the world is easy and things go smoothly in the beginning, but this will culminate in never-ending sorrow and suffering. We are free to choose one or the other.   Ammachi, *Awaken Children*, vol. 4, p. 117

If the outward path is the pursuit of happiness in anything that is outside of us, then the spiritual path is the pursuit of happiness in that which is inside of us. The spiritual path begins by first going within ourselves. In the end, this path will embrace everything, including the objects of the senses.

This causes us to ask why we must first look within if, after all, we find there is no difference between the inner and the outer. In our present state of mind there is only the outer. We do not see the essential or inner nature of all things. Because of this we make bad decisions and suffer as a result. There is a secret door that will lead us out of the delusion of duality-only, and that secret door is in our own hearts. We must make the effort to walk out of the maze in order to realize it was a maze.

Sri Adi Shankara (born 686 C.E.) articulates this in his threefold axiom that states:

1. The world is unreal.
2. God is real.
3. God is the world.

In step one we have the feeling that there must be more to existence than eating, procreating, and acquiring. We feel there is something phony or unreal about all of this. At this point our perception of the world as duality-only, or as something separate from our Self, is an illusion.

Thus, "the world is unreal." In the second step, we turn toward God (literally Brahman in the original text). We seek God in the most accessible place that is within ourselves. We come to an understanding of the reality of God.

In the third step, we see our own essential nature and thereby realize that it is the same essential nature of all things. Thus God is the world. To see another person and to also see that they are a manifestation of God is the result. The same is true for objects. How does step three occur?

Arriving at the center of being is like climbing to the peak of a mountain. From the mountain top we can see 360 degrees, and we understand that all of the various environments, forests, oceans, deserts, are part of the same landscape. In the same way, arriving at the center of all being, we see this essential awareness as life, light, and love (God) flowing out to all of creation, constantly sustaining and informing it. From the center, we can look out to anyone or anything and see the flow of this essential being streaming out into the diverse manifestations of the world.

From this point of view everything exists as a single unity. Therefore, God is the world.

> And when he was demanded of the Pharisees, when the kingdom of God should come, he answered them and said, "The kingdom of God cometh not with observation: Neither shall they say, Lo here! or, lo there! for, behold, the kingdom of God is within you." Luke 17:20-21, KJV

The outward path is, at first glance, inviting, seductive, and easily engaged. In contrast, the spiritual path will appear, at first, to be foreign, abstract, irrelevant, bitter, and difficult. The spiritual path requires constant self-examination, alertness, discipline, and control of the mind, while surrendering the self, the ego and all its desires, delusions, and fantasies. The outward path requires dullness, sloth, and failure to examine our lives. The spiritual path requires that we ask difficult questions such as, "Who am I?" and "Why am I here?" The outward path requires only that we ask, "How can I be comfortable and get more pleasure?" In the end, the outward path yields the bitter fruit of sorrow and suffering, while the spiritual path leads us to endless fields of love, peace, and happiness.

No Guarantees

These days the only friend that is faultless
Is a bottle of red wine and a book of poems.

Wherever you are going, go alone, for the road to enlighten-
    ment is
very narrow and full of curves. And take your wineglass
    with you, for there are no guarantees.

I am not the only writer that is worried about having a job.
Knowledge without experience is the "wise man's" fate.

In this noisy street, the voice of reason says:
The world and all its possessions is not security.

Let me tell you an old story: the face of an old camel,
    destined by
Fate to be black, cannot become white from washing and
    cleaning.

Everything you see around you will one day disappear,
Except Love, which lasts forever.

I had great hopes that, with my heart, I would unite with
    You.
But along the Road of Life, death lurks like highway
    robbery.

I say hold on to the Moon-Faced One's hair, and don't tell a
   soul!
For the effect of Saturn and the stars, is agony and good luck.

No one will ever see Hafiz sober, never.
He is drunk on the wine of endless Eternity, and keeps asking for more!

> Hafiz, *Drunk on the Wine of the Beloved - 100 Poems of Hafiz*,
> translated by Thomas Rain Crowe, Shambala Publications, Inc.

THE EGO

What is the ego? The ego is devoted to me… me… me… while
love is devoted to you…you…you…. The ego and love are mutu-
ally exclusive. Like oil and water, they won't mix.

> God will not reside where there is ego and selfishness. If
> these are there, God will move a thousand feet away from
> us. He will come close if we call sincerely.
> Ammachi, *Awaken Children, vol. II,* p. 343

The ego is the part of our psyche that clings to the outward path and
shuns the inward path. The outward path maintains the ego's
pseudo-reality by virtue of its identification with objects. The inward path leads to oneness or unification with all of life, and that
view diminishes the ego. The ego is the idea that we exist indepen-
dently and separately from God, from each other, and from all of
life. The ego makes each person into an island, surrounded and protected by a moat of fear and narrowness of mind that loathes anything that is different from his or her own self-described menu of
human existence. This makes it very difficult to find persons who
are interested in getting rid of the ego.

> Everyone wants to keep their ego, it is so precious to them.
> People think that the ego is an embellishment; it is not con-
> sidered to be a burden anymore. People do not feel the
> heaviness of their ego. They feel comfortable inside its
> small, hard shell. They feel afraid and insecure to come out
> of it. They think that they are well protected where they are.

> For them, what lies beyond the shell of their ego is frighten-
> ing, it is unknown and therefore unsafe. They believe that
> what lies beyond their ego is not for them, it is meant only
> for those who are not capable of doing anything else.
>
> Ammachi, *Awaken Children*, vol. VII, p. 159

The ego arises out of identification with the body and the simple observation that bodies appear to be separate entities. If we have the
feeling, "I am the body," then we must also feel that we are separate
from everyone else. This would be expected, because the five
senses tell us that all bodies are separate objects. The mind's identification with the body gives rise to the thought of being an individual. The root of this "individual" is what we call the original
"I-thought." Which came first, the illusory I-thought which generated a body for its expression, or did the body come first, thus giving
rise to the I-thought as the logical extension of its separateness?
Who can say?

The ego is an illusion like a mirage in the desert. This truth has been
scientifically demonstrated by Bell's Theorem. Bell's Theorem reveals that all objects in the universe are connected. All objects, and
that includes our bodies, are simultaneously affecting all other objects. Bell's Theorem states that objects have no localized existence,
meaning they do not stand alone as separate entities. Everything is
connected and is part of a "whole" like a big bowl of cosmic gelatin.
If we poke it on one side, it wiggles on the other. Bell's Theorem has
been scientifically demonstrated in the laboratory and is no longer
subject to debate. The fact that we are all connected and not separate is now indisputable. If this is true, then our ego, or sense of
separateness, is not real. This is hard to grasp, not because the concept is difficult, but because it is so contrary to our everyday view of
reality. Our collective psyche had the same problem when it was
discovered that the earth revolved around the sun and not vice versa.
The perception was far removed from the reality and most could not
and would not believe it.

Let's take a look at how the ego works. The I-thought attaches to
the body. This gives rise to the illusion of its existence, but it only
begins there. The I-thought then produces the mind in the way that

most of us experience it. From the egoistic point of view, everything is understood to exist or be defined as it relates to our I-thought. Each ego is constantly chanting the mantra, "It's all about ME." Each ego becomes the subject of everything that happens. This "center of existence" feeling may be buried several layers deep, but it will be found at the core of our perception of the world. For example, one country may threaten our country. This creates a sense of indignation and rejection of the threat. On the surface it seems we are doing this out of love for our country. That is the top layer. Underneath, we find that our "love for our country" is formed from the ego's use of nationality to define itself. The threat to our country is also a threat to our ego.

At the deepest level of this egoistic perception, we find the origin of the primal concept or thought of a "world." This "world" appears to exist outside of ourselves (outside the body). We see the world as separate from ourselves by assigning the world and all its objects a relationship to our I-thought. We are like a storekeeper (ego) that does business with a constant stream of customers (the world), separated by the shop display-counter of deals, relationships, and transactions. We see ourselves as individuals that are carried through the bazaars of the world's experiences in the palanquin of the brain. Or, we are like the pilots of WWII army tanks with two-inch steel armor plating. We are constantly peering out onto our battlefield from the observation slits of the eyes and the other senses, while constantly pulling levers that move the arms and legs and other motorized aspects of our tanks. We perceive that we are inside the body and the world is outside the body. This is all delusional and created by the illusory I-thought.

Legions of personal definitions further enhance the presence of the I-thought. Name, status, IQ, nationality, religion, temperament, political affiliation, race, food preferences, relationship to others, favorite football team, belonging to a group, being a hater of someone, and other personal definitions dangle from our I-thought like ornaments on a Christmas tree. Our ego could be John Doe, middle aged, 30 pounds overweight, superior to people in group A, inferior to people in group B, a Denver Broncos fan, a blue-collar worker, possessed of a temper problem which he is not about to try to control because that's "just who he is," a lover of potatoes, a hater of cabbage, asthmatic, a white Anglo-Saxon Protestant, and the lord and master of a family consisting of a wife and two children.

The ego can also adopt subservient identities wherein it is always the victim and is wrapped in a security blanket of self-pity. There is no shortage of identities the ego may adopt. We pin these badges on ourselves with great satisfaction and comfort, otherwise we fear that we will be hopelessly lost and adrift in a dark sea of ungrounded anonymity. To the ego, this fear arises from the horror of a perceived possibility of non-existence, or "I-am-not." The ego is directly defined by these personal preferences and aversions. Any contradiction is threatening and invokes fear.

The ego is an imaginary line drawn in the sand of our mind. Imagine a map of the United States. Now, imagine our own state and look at the outline of it. If we were to physically get in a car and drive to a point where our state borders another state, we would not find our line. It exists in our minds and, by extension, on the map, but it is not real.

Armed with a multitude of preconceptions, likes, and dislikes, we overlay our personal identities, attachments, and aversions onto the world, others, and God, just like the lines we use to define the states on a map. Our own ego is like a clear piece of plastic (the I-thought) on which we have drawn many lines (the identities, attachments and aversions). It is a template of self-imposed definitions that we unconsciously overlay onto the pure presence of life. Thus, the mind filters and interprets our experiences according to our own self-constructed template. Nothing is left to direct experience. Our existence revolves in the cocoon of this dreamlike state of being, which will easily be out of harmony with the greater universal order. We are hallucinating. Validity is granted to our delusions of separation when we see so many others having a similar hallucination.

Thus far, our discussion about the ego has been primarily academic. In actual practice, it is too much to expect the ego to disappear right away.

> It is true that one or two can get rid of the 'I' through samadhi; but these cases are very rare. You may indulge in thousands of reasonings, but still the 'I' comes back. You may cut the peepal-tree to the very root today, but you will

notice a sprout springing up tomorrow. Therefore if the 'I'
must remain, let the rascal remain as the 'servant I'. As long
as you live, you should say, 'O God, Thou art the Master
and I am 'Thy servant.' The 'I' that feels 'I am the servant
of God, I am His devotee' does not injure one.

Ramakrishna, *The Gospel of Ramakrishna*, p. 170,
translated by Swami Nikhilananda.

ONE THREAD OF SWEETNESS

Compassionate Divine Mother
There is nothing of my own
   that I can give you
      that is worth even a single moment
         of your immaculate vision

If only I were your proud and victorious warrior son
   returning from the triumphant conquest of the ego,
      I would happily lay the spoils of war
      and the treasures of a vanquished foe
         at your royal feet

Then I would certainly be worthy of your divine touch

But I am still a small child
   with only a wooden stick for a sword
      and the ego is an ancient foe
      that I have yet to subdue

Nor has this mind become the still, calm lake
   upon which your reflection is clearly seen

The desires of the body
   and the roar of incessant thoughts
   are a bully that, when challenged,
      still pushes this child
      face first into the mud

And I still become angered and react foolishly
   and attachments still bind these arms and legs
      preventing me from climbing

your snow-capped mountain peaks
of transcendent awareness

Having been defeated again and again
I have no trophies to offer you

Mother of light
have compassion on this small child
who has failed to rein in
the wild-eyed galloping horses
of birth and death

Yet there is one thread of sweetness left unbroken
on this smoldering battlefield
in which the forces of light and darkness
play out their destiny

That thread to which I desperately cling
is my love for you

Hold me in your arms, sweet Mother
and tell me that you love me
and that you want me to be by your side
without regard for my many failures

You are my eternal Beloved
and this single thread of sweetness
we will weave into a universe of shining love

From the book, *Soft Moon Shining*, by Ethan Walker III

All of the afflictive emotions such as greed, hatred, jealousy, and arrogance are the products of the ego. This becomes self-evident if one courageously examines the source of these emotions. Having grasped the magnitude of trouble and suffering that is delivered to us by the ego, we will be inspired to at least reduce its influence.

Two Paths

The central purpose of any spiritual path is to subdue or remove the illusion of the ego so that God or Self can be realized. The goal is not to gain God or attain God, because that would imply that at one time God was not present. God is always here and now, but this truth is hidden because we see "through a glass darkly" (Corinthians 13:12). The goal is to realize God, and this can only happen to the degree to which the ego is diminished.

When the obscuring power of the ego is gone, God is revealed as the transcendent and immanent luminescent reality of infinite love. Then compassion will naturally and effortlessly flow from our hearts like a great endless river.

With regard to the spiritual path, there are essentially two ways that we may go to reduce or remove the ego. One is the path of knowledge of the Self (in Sanskrit, "jnana" or knowledge[2]), and the other is the path of devotion to God (in Sanskrit, "bhakti" or devotion). When we ask the question, "What is all of this?" we find two ways to approach the answer. They are really two sides of the same coin. Each path leads to the other, and in the end both are seen as the same. The path of Self-knowledge is peace: formless, impersonal, and focused on the universal Self that contains everything. The path of devotion is love: infinite form, personal, and focused on God who is in everything. With knowledge the truth is transcendent, and with devotion the truth is immanent. One who follows the path of knowledge calls the truth the Self. One who follows the path of devotion calls the truth God. One who has reached the goal in either path will see no difference.

Question: Mother, which is best, devotion or knowledge?

Amma: Devotion fortified with knowledge is what is needed. Look at the tree and the creeper. If the tree is not there, the creeper will not grow upwards. You should approach jnana through bhakti. Bhakti which is not based on essential principles (tattwas) will only help to bind one. That is harmful. There are certain creepers that keep the trees completely bound. Likewise, bhakti without jnana will only help one to get bound more and more. Jnana means to

---

[2] More than book knowledge; rather the direct intuiting of Reality. Also the same concept of gnosis to early Gnostic Christians.

grow straight upwards. Tattwa bhakti is that which embraces jnana tightly. Then it will not come down.

Bhakti and jnana, though seemingly different, are not two. Bhakti is the means and jnana the end. Bhakti without jnana and jnana without bhakti are both harmful. In fact, bhakti is the easiest and least complicated way. Anyone and everyone can follow it. Bhakti culminates in jnana. The Lord of a true devotee and Brahman, the Absolute Reality of the Jnani, are really one and the same. Bhakti is usually prescribed for people who are predominantly emotional, and jnana for intellectuals. Jnana without bhakti is dry, and bhakti without jnana is blind.   Ammachi, *Awaken Children*, vol. II, p. 287-288

Amma is saying that practicing the path of Self-knowledge or jnana without love and devotion is difficult because it is dry. Motivation to discipline one's self without love and devotion is tedious, tends to reside in the realm of the intellect, and can lead to pride and arrogance. If there is love and devotion in the practice of jnana, motivation comes more easily and the ego is subdued. Conversely, if one practices devotion without the underlying awareness of the universal all-pervading nature of God or Self that is behind the form of one's devotion, then a selfish relationship may ensue which can evolve into narrow mindedness and an arrogant tendency to exclude other religions, paths, and forms claiming, "My way is the only way."

Earlier, we explored the idea that the goal of spiritual practice is not so much the attainment of something but rather is to get rid of something. This "something" to be dropped is the ego or sense of separateness that we can fundamentally describe as the concept of "I" and "mine." Separateness[3] prevents jnana or direct knowledge because our sense of separateness blinds us to the reality that there is only one Self. How can we begin to entertain the concept of "one Self" if we are absorbed in the feeling that we are separate from everyone else? At first glance, we will laugh at the very idea.

Separateness blocks love, because each is the antithesis of the other. The result of love will be to merge in the Beloved, whereas separate-

---

[3] In Sanskrit *avidya* or primal ignorance.

ness will not merge in anything simply because it is separate. When we love, we are focused on God or "others" and what we can do for them. In this way our sense of isolation subsides. We feel unified in the radiance of love. These gears turn the other way when we become absorbed in our own separateness, which causes love to flee from us like a rabbit being chased by a hungry coyote. When the sense of separateness is dropped, the timeless reality of love and one Self remains as it always has been. So, the goal of knowledge or devotion is the same: to eliminate that aspect of our mind which hides the Infinite Presence.

THE PATH OF KNOWLEDGE - JNANA

The philosophy of jnana, aka Vedanta (from the 5,000-year-old scriptures called the Vedas) or advaita (Sanskrit meaning "not two" or nonduality), has become quite popular in recent years, especially through the recorded dialogs of Sri Ramana Maharshi and Sri Nisargadatta Maharaj. Both of these great saints left this world a number of years ago (1950 and 1981, respectively). Jnana begins with the supposition that in all eternity there is only one formless indescribable Self, or pure awareness, that animates and informs all beings. In fact, all beings are varying forms or expressions of this singular pure awareness. The philosophy of jnana states that our own existence is all that is self-evident, and by inquiring into the nature of this "I AM" we will eventually arrive at the truth of the one universal Self. The "I" that is in me is one and the same as the "I" that is in you. The practice primarily consists of meditating on, or seeking to know, the source of the "I" and a fearless examination and subsequent elimination of all that we find not to be our Self. We are encouraged to see ourselves as simply the witnesses of events, as though sitting in a movie theater.

The path of jnana is very satisfying to the intellect. We are engrossed in the idea that what we see as the world and ourselves is an illusion, and so we are intellectually transported from our habitual way of perceiving the world and ourselves. We are charged with an emerging excitement as our mind momentarily escapes the gravity of our conventional life. However, jnana is much more than this, and it is very easy to confuse intellectual titillation with depth of perception.

The philosophy of jnana is very simple, but we may miss the fine print that reads: it is very difficult to be simple. It is easy to mistake intellectual perception for true knowledge. Left unguided, this can promote an attitude of laziness and spiritual pride in which we take the position that there is no need to do any spiritual practice because we already are "THAT." In the book *Zen Mind Beginner's Mind*, Suzuki Roshi counters this avenue of thought by saying that, paradoxically, we must make an effort to become effortless.

Jnana that is caught in the intellectual web will expand the ego with pride. We begin to enjoy the feeling of "knowing something" that no one else knows. It is so easy for us to unknowingly make these errors. The ego begins to feel special and subsequently adopts an attitude of arrogance with regard to other practices. We will not stop to question the fact that we still get upset if someone yells at us or calls us an abusive name. We will close our eyes to the confounding question that lurks in the back of our mind, "If there is only one Self, then who is there to get mad at whom?" Cornered by this line of questioning, we may mistakenly claim that all such emotional afflictions and deviant behavior are the activity of the one Self. Amma answers a question from a woman:

> Mother: Daughter, jnana marga is good, but very few can follow it correctly. If a real Guru is there, one can travel the path of knowledge. When the ego arises in the disciple, the Guru understands it and immediately corrects him. The disciple will not swerve from the path. If there is no Guru he will think, "I am Brahman. I can do anything, I have no attachment to anything" and he will be ready to make any mistake.
>
> A person who accepts the path of knowledge without having a Guru is like one who studies for an M.A. degree without attending the first grade.
>
> Ammachi, *Awaken Children*, vol. I, p. 143

There are many who talk about the path of knowledge. Mother has observed plenty of them. One sees no practice in action, only mere talk. They will say that everything is Brahman, the Absolute. If that is so, shouldn't they see others as one with themselves? But that is not usually the case. Those who are fit to walk in the path of knowledge will have a strong spiritual disposition inherited from the previous birth. The practice of knowledge is spontaneous for them. Others, in the name of knowledge, do nothing but babble and inflate their egos. They do harm to themselves and to others as well.

Ammachi, Awaken Children, vol. I, p. 189-190

The pitfalls leading to subtle ego expansion are so numerous and subtle that it renders the path of jnana impassable but for only a few.

Those who reach the Goal through the path of jnana can be counted on the fingers of your hand.

Ammachi, Eternal Wisdom, vol. II, p. 124

To know God through jnana and reasoning is extremely difficult. Ramakrishna, *The Gospel of Ramakrishna*, p. 94, translated by Swami Nikhilananda

THE PATH OF DEVOTION - BHAKTI

One of the teachers of the law came and heard them debating. Noticing that Jesus had given them a good answer, he asked him, "Of all the commandments, which is the most important?" "The most important one," answered Jesus, "is this: 'Hear, O Israel, the Lord our God, the Lord is one. Love the Lord your God with all your heart and with all your soul and with all your mind and with all your strength.' The second is this: 'Love your neighbor as yourself.' There is no commandment greater than these." "Well said, teacher," the man replied. "You are right in saying that God is one and there is no other but him. To love him with all your heart, with all your understanding and with all your strength, and to love your neighbor as yourself is more important than all burnt offerings and sacrifices." When Jesus saw that he had answered wisely, he said to him, "You are not far from the kingdom of God."   Mark 12:28-34, NIV

Traveling the path of a devotee has many advantages. For the purpose of this discussion, devotion means pure love for God and not simply a sense of duty or supplication to God to fulfill our desires. Here, devotion or bhakti means pure selfless love[4].

Before we continue with this section, we should be forewarned that the mind does not easily accept the concept of love as a spiritual path. In John 1:5 we read, "The light shines in the darkness, but the darkness has not understood it." This could just as easily read, "Love shines all about but the ego-centered mind does not understand it." The mind wants bobbles of identity–toys to play with–in the form of far ranging concepts, intricate definitions, multi-layered fields of energy, stratospheric philosophies, and interpenetrating planes of consciousness, all carefully cataloged and displayed like vacation brochures at a travel agency. These beckon the restless and bored mind to experience fantastic lights and altered states of being. All of this should be endlessly articulated in volumes of writings and esoteric road maps to the Beyond.

Because of this mental restlessness, most of us have forgotten how to love. Our intellects have grown while our hearts have shriveled into small black stones. For most of us, love is nothing more than a four-letter word leaving us with little context or appreciation for the idea of love as a spiritual path. If someone says the word "love," there is no reaction. If someone says "free buffet" or "hot stock tip," we glow like a neon sign. If one could but once taste the sweetness of God–weep for God with streaming tears of pure innocent love falling from blushing cheeks–Oh!…Oh!…Oh!

> In the state of pure innocent love, the lover is always hungry. He wants to eat up his beloved. There is an insatiable hunger in pure love. One can see and experience this intense hunger even in worldly love. But in spiritual love the intensity reaches its peak. That apex is the extreme point, the ultimate limit which is limitless, for this love is all-expansive. In a true seeker this love becomes like a forest fire, yet it is even more intense, more consuming. His whole being will burn with the intensity of that fire of love. In that blazing fire he himself gets consumed and then comes the complete merging.
> Ammachi, *Awaken Children*, vol. IV, p. 39

[4] In Sanskrit pure selfless love for God is *prema bhakti* but in this book, and for simplification, the word bhakti will mean the same.

RIVER OF TEARS

My Beloved!
A great miracle is happening!
  The world of the many is dissolving
  like so many chocolate candy kisses
      held tightly in a child's hand!

We are alone at last you and I.
You are my infinite companion, my precious, my unspeak-
              able beauty,
  my compassionate and adorable One!

As you hold me in your arms
  and I whisper softly, "I love you" again and again and again,
  my heart becomes a torrential river of love
      giving rise to tears of unimaginable joy
          falling one by one
              from my blushing cheeks

From the book, *Soft Moon Shining* by Ethan Walker III

DEVOTION IS SIMPLE

The first point we will consider is the simplicity of devotion.

> Children, as far as Mother is concerned, the path of devotion
> is the best and the easiest since most people are predomi-
> nately emotional in nature. Not only that, bhakti marga
> (path of devotion) has no complications like the other paths.
> There are no harmful techniques or complications involved
> in love. Simply love the Lord. Love is not aggressive; it is
> a constant flow. Ammachi, *Awaken Children*, vol. III, p. 101

> But generally speaking, the Path of Devotion is the easiest
> and the least complicated. While anybody can love, not all
> can do pranayama (breath control) or Hatha Yoga (yogic
> postures). Only certain people endowed with a certain men-
> tal and physical constitution can do these. But love has no
> prerequisites. Whoever has a heart can love, and everyone
> has a heart. To love is an innate tendency in human beings.

However, we cannot say that pranayama or Hatha Yoga come naturally to human beings. Bhakti is love – loving God, loving your own Self, and loving all beings.

Ammachi, *Awaken Children*, vol. IV, p. 143

Amma is saying that there is no price of admission to the school of love. It's the "people's path"– the path to God for anyone. We do not have to possess any special skills or talents to walk this way. Every human being has all the necessary equipment to love and to realize God through love, and that is astonishing good news! No one is excluded! The practice of love automatically induces subtlety of mind, sensitivity to vibrations, raising of the kundalini, humility, concentration, meditation, bliss, and all of the experiences regarded as mileposts on the spiritual journey. Love for God does all these things quite naturally and spontaneously, without any thought on the part of the practitioner. The devotee who is absorbed in love has little or no interest in these things beyond a passing curiosity. The Beloved is the all-in-all. Even thoughts of liberation and enlightenment are discarded like so many old clothes thrown carelessly to the ground as one dives head first into the ocean of love. The devotee does not care for himself or enlightenment but only for God. The fire of love further consumes notions of egocentricity and that age-old whine, "What's in it for me?"

DEVOTION DESTROYS THE SELF-CENTERED EGO

Love can easily consume your ego.

Ammachi, *Awaken Children*, vol. IV, p. 39

Pure love removes all negative feelings. Destroying all selfishness, it expects nothing but gives everything. Pure love is a constant giving up – giving up of everything that belongs to you. What really belongs to you? Only the ego. Love consumes in its flames all preconceived ideas, prejudices and judgments, all those things which stem from the ego. Pure love is nothing but the emptying of the mind of all its fears and the tearing off of all masks. It exposes the Self as it is.

For the lover to wholeheartedly receive and welcome the beloved, pure love prepares the mind by chasing away all the enemies of love. This results in a constant flow of the lover's heart towards the beloved. There is an unquenchable thirst to drink in the beloved, an unappeasable hunger to eat him up and an immeasurable intensity to become love. It is the death of the ego to live in love. But once you attain unity with the beloved, then there is only peace, love, light and silence. All conflicts end and you shine forth in the radiance of Supreme Love. In order to attain this highest kind of love one has to undergo some pain. But that pain is not pain when you consider the unending flow of bliss which you are going to gain when you reach the goal.

Ammachi, *Awaken Children*, vol. IV, p. 246

We have enshrined the ego as the center of our existence. Our decisions are based on a self-serving creed of action that admits no others, acknowledges no others, and serves no others. If an action doesn't further our own self-interest, then it is not worth considering.

For example, we find a person to marry because we expect the other person to satisfy our needs like a milk cow gives milk. Swami Vivekananda called this "shopkeeper's love;" we will only love someone if we think we will get something in exchange. We encourage our children to do well in school because they are extensions of our own egos and if they do well, we also do well by proxy. The point here is to understand the nature of the ego and how its self-centered way of acting is thoroughly ingrained and habitual. It is so deep and so ancient that we are not aware of its process. However, with a little observation, the ego can clearly be seen for what it is. We simply need to become aware of it.

Love, on the other hand, erases this habitual self-centered line of thinking. Pure love asks nothing in return and performs acts of compassion and kindness without the preponderate weight of self-interest. Love does not seek the welfare of one's own self, but rather the well-being of others. Love is not absorbed in the narcissistic fascination with one's own ego but is absorbed in fascination with God. Love peels back the curtain of blindness and reveals the unspeakable beauty that radiates from the core of all things. Love reaches out to God and to others, while the ego withdraws into its shell of bobbles and trinkets. Love sees others as brothers and sisters, while the ego sees others as objects of fear or opportunity.

Other paths may enshrine the idea of attaining enlightenment, liberation, or salvation. The lover-of-God is not interested in these things and is content to be in any state of mind the Lord wills, as long as he or she is not deprived of the opportunity to love God. This contentment cultivates an attitude of acceptance for the events in our life, whether good or bad. Everything is accepted as God's will. Devotees pray for constant remembrance of God, not because they want something for themselves, but because they are absorbed in their love for the Divine. For devotees, thoughts of enlightenment are of no concern. Love-intoxicated souls will pray, "Lord, do anything you want with me, but don't take away my love for you." At first glance it may seem this is a self-serving request. However, the very nature of love is for others and God as opposed to "I and mine."

We remove a habit by replacing it with another habit. We replace the habit of our ego-centered point of view with the habit of love. Therefore, the practice of devotion or pure love for God will remove the ego.

AUTUMN LEAVES

Red, yellow, and brown leaves curled by autumn's first frost
      float like an armada of great ships
      in the winding brook

They celebrate by dancing in the playful current
      for soon they will arrive
      at the ocean of endless love

From the book, *Soft Moon Shining* by Ethan Walker III

DEVOTION IS POWERFUL

Spiritual progress on the path of love is rapid, because the intensity of emotion creates powerful concentration. Progress is deep and quick.

Crying to God for five minutes is equal to one hour of meditation.   Ammachi, *Awaken Children*, vol. 2, p. 331

An emotion is simply a powerful, continuous, one-pointed thought. A well-developed emotional wellspring is essential to personal creativity. Albert Einstein was passionate and emotional about the nature of the universe, which gave him the one-pointedness and concentration necessary to unlock some of nature's deepest mysteries. We all enjoy watching the passion of a conductor or a rock star who pours his being into the nuances of his musical joy. Drama, music, art, and poetry move us if there is passion behind the presentation.

> If a person excels in singing, music, dancing, or any other art,
> he can also quickly realize God provided he strives sincerely.
> Ramakrishna, *Gospel of Ramakrishna*,
> p. 427, translated by Swami Nikhilananda

What Sri Ramakrishna says is true, because a well-developed emotional nature is required to excel in any of the arts, and that same emotional nature will enable us to quickly realize God. God is not to be gained through reasoning. God is something we feel. God dwells in the realm of the heart.

If we are not now an artisan, we should not despair. With a little work and God's grace, anyone can cultivate a feeling nature.

Devotion Invokes Grace

Grace, the most important aspect of our practice, is granted according to the depth of our sincere love for God.

> Constant remembrance of God, irrespective of time and place,
> is real devotion. If you practice in this manner, He will come;
> He must come. God will come and play with you."
> Ammachi, *Awaken Children*, vol. III, p. 320

God cannot refrain from responding to our sincere love, tears, and prayers. God is like a mother who cannot and will not turn away from the love of one of her children. In the following excerpt from Chapter 12 in the Bhagavad Gita, Lord Krishna reveals the power of devotion to his friend Arjuna:

> Arjuna said: So between those who are ever-disciplined,
> who are devoted to you and attend on you, and those who

pursue the imperishable unmanifest, who are the most expert in yoga[5]?

The Lord said: I consider the most expert in yoga to be those who, ever-disciplined, having fixed their minds on me, attend on me filled with the highest faith.

Yet those who attend on the indefinable, imperishable unmanifest, ubiquitous and inconceivable, unchanging, un-moving, embedded,

Who controlling all their senses, are equably minded in all circumstances, and take pleasure in the welfare of all crea-tures, they too attain to me.

The barrier for those whose thoughts are attached to the unmanifest is greater, for it is not easy for the embodied to attain an unmanifest goal.[6]

But for those who resign every action to me, who, intent on me and meditating on me, with exclusive discipline worship me,

I am the one who rapidly hauls them out of the ocean of death and continual rebirth, Partha, for their thoughts are en-grossed in me.

> *The Bhagavad Gita*, translated by W.J. Johnson, Oxford
> University Press, Walton Street, Oxford, OX2 6DP

Sri Krishna, in the last sentence, speaking as God incarnate, states that he *quickly* saves the lovers of God from the ocean of birth and death.

DEVOTION BRINGS IMMEDIATE SATISFACTION

There is a benefit in following the path of devotion. One will get bliss from the very beginning itself. Thus one will be encouraged to perform sadhana [spiritual practices]. In other paths like pranayama (control of the breath), bliss will

---

[5] Yoga meaning union with God
[6] Sri Krishna comments on the difficulty of practicing jnana

be gained only at the end. Just as one gets fruit even from the base of a jackfruit tree, bhakti is the path from which one gets fruit from the very beginning onwards.

Ammachi, *Awaken Children*, vol. II, p. 345 [brackets by the author]

The state that we attain by calling and crying to God is equal to the bliss that the yogi experiences in samadhi.

Ammachi, *Awaken Children*, vol. III, p.320

Spiritual practice of any kind requires dedication and resolve. It is easier to maintain our motivation if there is some feedback along the way. The sense of ecstasy, the love and peace that we feel early in the path of devotion serves as encouragement. This positive imprinting helps the mind to ever increase its absorption in remembrance of God. It is like coaxing the cow into the barn with handfuls of sweet, new-mown hay as opposed to trying to beat it with a stick to get it to go into the barn. Because of this, our practice unfolds much more easily.

DEVOTION IS INNOCENCE

Children, the wonder and the love that you felt as a child will never return unless you can again play like a child. Innocence is within you, hidden deep inside. You have to rediscover it. And for this to happen, you must go deeper and deeper into your spiritual practices. When you can dive deep into your own consciousness, you will realize this innocence one day. At that moment you will discover the child within you. You will experience the innocence, the joy and the wonder that were hidden inside of you, and you will realize they were always there. You merely forgot your innocence for some time. It is as if you suddenly remember something after having forgotten about it for a very long time. That childlike innocence deep within you is God.

Ammachi, *Awaken Children*, vol. VI, p. 225

At that time the disciples came to Jesus and asked, "Who is the greatest in the kingdom of heaven?" He called a little child and had him stand among them. And he said: "I tell you the truth, unless you change and become like little chil-

dren, you will never enter the kingdom of heaven. Therefore, whoever humbles himself like this child is the greatest
in the kingdom of heaven.   Matthew 18:1-4, NIV

The grace of God is gained by innocence. In truth, God's grace is
always there, but we unwittingly close the door through negative
egoistic attitudes. That is why Jesus says we have to be like a little
child in order to enter the kingdom of heaven (Matthew 8:3). When
spiritual experiences happen, pride comes sniffing around like a
back-alley tomcat seeking his fragrant paramour. The ego is sorely
tempted to feel somehow responsible for the insight or experience.
It begins to imagine that it must have been a great spiritual person in
past lives, otherwise, how could it have the insight to have arrived at
these extraordinary experiences. It never asks how the "great practitioner" in the past life got its initial grace. The ego takes notice that
most others are not having these experiences. "I must be special,"
the ego reasons. This struggle with pride is quite common. It is also
difficult to overcome. Most of us never see pride coming. It sneaks
up with a baseball bat in its hand, ready to knock us off our meditation seat and into the next county. It is difficult to know when pride
has devoured our innocence.

The practice of devotion continuously places us in a position of humility. By practicing love for God, we are able to hold on to the
soul-preserving thought that all we are and all we have is from God
and God alone. Love for God is that life preserver filled with the
atmosphere of humility. As our dependence on God and God's love
expands, we can begin to grasp the idea that we are utterly helpless
like small kittens. We are able to pull this dependence on God out of
our bag like a magic potion each time the demon of pride comes
calling. We place our love for God around our psyche like a mantle
of invisibility, so that pride will fail to find us and seduce us. Love
for God compassionately transforms us from great spiritual aspirants
into small helpless children–God's children.

What is that innocence that love reveals? We are blessed if we can
still remember what it felt like to be a small child. Then we can
rummage through the attic of our distant childhood memories and
resurrect the incredible lightness of being we felt before the heavy
weight of the ego descended upon us, smothering the last flickering

flame of innocence. If we are not able to remember our innocence, we shouldn't despair. Love will bring it back.

> My sweet Lord
> Hm, my Lord
> Hm, my Lord
> I really want to see you
> Really want to be with you
> Really want to see you Lord
> But it takes so long, my Lord
>
> My sweet Lord
> Hm, my Lord
> Hm, my Lord
>
> I really want to know you
> Really want to go with you
> Really want to show you Lord
> That it won't take long, my Lord (hallelujah)
>
> Lyrics from the song *My Sweet Lord* by George Harrison
> on the album *All Things Must Pass*

STRINGS IN THE TAPESTRY OF DEVOTION

Jesus also proposed the practice of devotion. Jesus had two commandments for us: love God and love our neighbor. He states this several times in the gospels.

> Teacher, which is the greatest commandment in the Law?
>
> Jesus replied: Love the Lord your God with all your heart and with all your soul and with all your mind. This is the first and greatest commandment. And the second is like it: Love your neighbor as yourself. All the Law and the Prophets hang on these two commandments.
>
> Matthew 22:36-40, NIV

Our discussion will primarily revolve around commandment number one. Commandment number two is commandment number one applied to the world, in which everyone and everything is the incarnation of the Divine. We should note that Jesus did not simply say, "love God." Rather, he was quite emphatic and dramatic. He asked us to love the Lord our God with all our heart and with all our soul and with all our strength and with all our mind. He is telling us to pour all our heart, our emotion, our resolve, and our thoughts into it. Jesus is like a good basketball coach that grips his team by the proverbial shoulders, looks them straight in the eye, and with all the emotion and intensity he can muster says, "You've got to give this your very best effort! You've got to pour every ounce of your heart into it!"

> The small heart should become bigger and bigger and, eventually, totally expansive. A spark can become a forest fire. So to have only a spark is enough, for the spark is also fire. Keep blowing on it, fanning it. Sooner or later it will burn like a forest fire, sending out long tongues of flame. At present, love is like a spark within us. Constantly blow on it, using the fan of the Divine Name, japa and meditation. You may perspire, sneeze and cough, but do not stop. Your body may become hot; tears may fill your eyes; you may want to faint. But do not stop. If you perspire, you sneeze and cough, persist in your efforts, and be assured then that you are heading towards the goal. Soon you will become Love itself. This is the reward for your love.
>
> Ammachi, *Awaken Children*, vol. IV, p. 143

DOES GOD EXIST?

> Student: It is said that there is a God but I am unable to believe that.

> Mother: Children, to say that there is no God is like saying "I have no tongue" with your own tongue. Is it possible for a person who has no tongue to say "I have no tongue"? Likewise, when we say "There is no God," at that moment itself we agree that there is God. In order to say that a particular object is 'not,' we must have previously had a general knowledge of that object. How can we prove the nonexistence of something which is not known to us? Truth is only one. That is God. God-Realization is our life's aim.

Student: What is meant by God?

Mother: Son, if you can answer the questions which Mother is going to ask, Mother will tell you what God is.

Student: All right, I will answer.

Mother: Son, what did you eat this morning?

Student: I ate dosa1.

Mother: What other dish was there with it?

Student: Chutney.

Mother: What was it made of?

Student: Coconut.

Mother: Where did you get the coconut from?

Student: From a coconut tree.

Mother: Where did the coconut tree come from?

Student: From a coconut.

Mother: Which was first, the coconut or the coconut tree? That is what Mother wants to know.

(The student sat tongue-tied.)

Mother: Son, why are you sitting silent? (Pause) Now, you should agree that there is a power beyond the coconut and the coconut tree which is the substratum of everything. That is God. A Unique Power which is inexpressible and beyond words. That is God. The First Cause for everything, that is what is known as God.

Student: It is easy to believe, when we are discussing the existence of a building or a coconut tree. But it is much more difficult to believe in something which we cannot see.

Mother: Son, would you feel angry if Mother asks you one thing?

Student: No.

Mother: Is your father still alive?

Student: Yes.

Mother: What about your father's father?

Student: He died long before my birth.

Mother: Do any grandchildren call their father a bastard because they have not seen their grandfather? Son, do you remember who gave birth to you? When you grew a little older everyone told you, "This is your mother." You believed it, even though you did not see the person when they gave birth to you. Do you believe it if someone says that there is cooking gas in cow dung? Cooking gas is not visible but gas can be extracted if one knows the technique. Often times it is blind faith that leads us to the goal. Son, suppose you left your house to come here. You got into the bus which comes here. Isn't it because of your faith that you will reach the destination? You got into the bus even though there are many vehicle accidents. Wasn't your expectation that you would reach here simply blind faith? Children, isn't it because of your blind faith that Mother will talk to you, and that you in turn will talk to Her? Children, all beliefs or faiths are blind.

Student: It is said that God is everywhere. If so, why is it necessary to go to particular places of worship?

Mother: There is wind everywhere but the person who comes to rest under a tree out of the scorching heat gets a special kind of rejuvenating coolness which filters through the leaves of the tree. Likewise, we can experience a unique peace when we go to Mahatmas. The significance of going to other places of worship is also the same. The atmosphere in a temple and a liquor shop are different, aren't they?

Student: Mother, how can we see God?

Mother: Children, when there is good sunlight we can see numerous dust particles in the ray of sunlight which enters the room through a small hole in the roof of the house. Due to the lack of concentrated light, it is not seen in other places. Our mind is very dim. It has no subtlety. Just like charging a battery, through subtlety we illumine our mind, we can see God. Having searched with our external eyes, do not say, "I am not seeing God, therefore I don't believe in God." We should not make a big fuss saying, "I will only believe in the things that I see." Search, certainly you can see.

Without God's Grace, we cannot see Him. If we want to get His Grace, the ego in us should go. The well might say, "Everyone is drinking water from me. If I am not here, how will they cook food?" But the well does not know that it was dug by someone and that the bricks which make it beautiful were made by somebody else. Our situation is also the same. We become egotistical thinking that "I am greater than everything else." But even to move a finger we need God's power. (Pointing Her finger at a distance) However powerful a cyclone is, it cannot do anything to that blade of grass. Whereas the huge trees standing with their heads high will be uprooted. All grace will flow to us if a servant-like attitude (dasa bhavana or attitude of humility) comes to us. After that, nothing can move us. But God will not abide where there is ego. We will be uprooted by the cyclone of ego."

Ammachi, *Awaken Children*, vol. I, p. 1

GOD PERSONALIZED

The practice of devotion requires that we embrace a personalized form of God. This can be difficult if we have only the intellect with which to work. Many think the idea of God having a personal relationship with us is antiquated and simpleminded, like the Santa Claus we once accepted as real when we were children, only to discover later that it had all been a charade. The intellect can more easily accept God to be energy or light. These are apparent. But to see that life is intelligent requires a subtle mind and an open heart – scarce commodities. While light or energy are truly forms of the one living God, they are not especially endearing to the heart in a personal way. It is difficult to feel we are hugging energy and to feel that energy is hugging us. It is too impersonal and mechanical.

We ourselves, as human beings, are proof that God can and does personalize. In the beginning there was only God. Where did God get the materials to construct the universe if there was only God? The answer is inescapable. Everything is made out of God. Everything about us is the manifestation of God stuff. When we walk and talk, it is because of God. It is God that is the power and awareness that reads and cognizes the words on this page. We might complain that our human forms are not permanent and thus cannot be the expression of a personal Absolute that must be permanent. One answer lies in considering that there is a single, personal Absolute that is the sum total of all forms, which includes our human forms. The personal Absolute does not depend on any particular form of existence but rather is simultaneously *all* forms of existence. What of this form-as-a-whole we might ask? Is it permanent? Is it absolute? Sri Adi Shankara (born 686 C.E.), who is widely regarded as the East Indian saint who gave birth to the current renaissance of non-dual philosophy, explains in his classic work *The Crest Jewel of Discrimination* that form (Maya) has no beginning. Therefore She is granted the status of Absolute.

> Maya, in her potential aspect, is the divine power of the Lord. She has no beginning. She is composed of the three gunas[7], subtle, beyond perception. It is from the effects she produces that her existence is inferred by the wise. It is she who gives birth to the whole universe.
>
> She is neither being nor non-being, nor a mixture of both. She is neither divided nor undivided, nor a mixture of both. She is neither an indivisible whole, nor composed of parts, nor a mixture of both. She is most strange. Her nature is inexplicable.
> Sri Adi Shankara, *Crest Jewel of Discrimination*, p 49, translated by Swami Prabhavananda and Christopher Isherwood, Vedanta Press

---

[7] Gunas – the three qualities of Nature which are: tamas, or ignorance and intertia; rajas, or delusion and activity; and sattva, or clarity and harmony.

In truth this "personalization" of the Absolute never happened, because it has always been so for all eternity. God is both form and formlessness; personal and impersonal–either will provide passage to the Supreme.

If we take the position that form was at one time willed into existence by the Absolute, we are faced with the problem of why or how the Absolute could suddenly disturb its emptiness by committing the finite act of willing anything. The only solution is to see that in reality there is no separating the Absolute (formless) from Nature (form) and vice versa. Everything is complete as it is, without beginning or end. Nothing was created and nothing will be destroyed. In the Heart Sutra we read that form is form, formlessness is formlessness, form is formlessness and formlessness is form. Both form and formlessness are paradoxically co-existent: God is both dual and non-dual in nature.

There is an intelligent principle that directs all forms, or we could say that all forms are the manifestation of this intelligent principle. It is this intelligent principle that will communicate directly with us in the practice of devotion. We may again ponder the magnitude of this and ask how such an intelligent principle can communicate with so many supplicants at the same time. How can God consciously direct the making of stars in the Eagle Nebula and, at the same time, have a conversation with us about the details of our own lives? God does this in the same way that a tree communicates with all of its leaves at the same time. The trunk and branches are conduits formed out of the formless itself. At the core of our tree is the "ocean of the formless" or pure conscious awareness which links all forms - the trunks and the branches – that arise out of it. Communication at this level, through the medium of the formless, is instantaneous, supraliminal – beyond the speed of light. Jesus expresses the truth that God is consciously omniscient:

> Are not five sparrows sold for two pennies? Yet not one of them is forgotten by God. Indeed, the very hairs of your head are all numbered.   Luke 12:6-7, NIV

This instantaneous connectivity is also driven home in quantum physics through Bell's Theorem, which we discussed previously in this book. How God does this is a mystery to us. Perhaps the universe is holographic, in which each part contains the sum of the whole. Indeed, the following prayer from the Vedas indicates exactly this idea.

> That is the Whole, this is the Whole;
> From the Whole, the Whole arises;
> Taking away the Whole from the Whole,
> The Whole remains.
>
> *Yajur Veda, Brhadaranyaka Upanishad*, 5.1

The purpose of this chapter has been to demonstrate that being devoted to the formless Absolute through one of its forms or manifestations, in no way compromises our acceptance of the formless Absolute. Ice may be sculpted into the form of a swan or an elephant, but the basic nature of either is still the same—ice. Regardless of whether we embrace the swan or the elephant, we have the same experience of "cold 'n wet." In the same way, we arrive at the essential nature of the Absolute, our own unborn, undying Self, by embracing any of its forms.

If we, as human beings, can profess intelligence, then we must at least admit that the universe that gave birth to us may also be endowed with intelligence.

THE RELATIONSHIP

According to classical Hindu scriptures on devotion, there are five fundamental devotional attitudes that one may assume in order to have a relationship with the Divine. It is not uncommon that our relationship may, at times, encompass or explore more than one avenue.

- Servant to master
- Friend to friend
- Child to parent
- Parent to child and
- Lover to beloved

In the attitude of servant to master, devotees express love with the heartfelt desire to be of service in some way to God. They set about doing God's work, expect nothing in return, and are simply joyous at having the opportunity to participate in God's plan. Hanuman had this attitude toward Rama.

In the attitude of friend to friend, devotees feel that God is their dearest friend, in whom they may confide their deepest secrets, concerns, and joys. Like two teenage girls staying up late at night talking about this and that, devotees feel that nothing is too small to discuss with the Lord. There is an intimate sharing at every level of their lives. Arjuna had this relationship to Krishna.

In the attitude of child to parent, devotees assume the attitude of small helpless children who are totally dependent on the Lord. In this mood, there is no joy greater than climbing onto the lap of God as would small children. Ammachi and Ramakrishna both practiced this relationship to the Divine Mother.

In the attitude of parent to child, devotees assume some responsibility for God. The idea is to attend to God, making sure God has enough to eat, making sure God does not get lost, and making sure God has good company. In this attitude, as with all of these approaches, the aim is to keep our mind on God, and it scarcely matters how this is accomplished. When the wandering Indian holy man Jatadhari came to Dakshineswar, he was engaged in this practice with the Boy Rama through the agency of a small metal image which he worshipped with the utmost reverence. Sri Ramakrishna also became engaged with Ramlala (Boy Ram) for a period and a fascinating account of this is given on page 107 of *Ramakrishna and His Disciples* by Christopher Isherwood. Also, the same parent to child relationship can be seen in the worship of the baby Krishna. Many devotees of Ammachi carry Amma dolls to the same end.

In the attitude of lover to beloved, devotees feel as though they are married to God. God is seen as the eternal spouse. Men marry the eternal in the form of a goddess and may see themselves as betrothed to Goddess aspects such as Kali, Durga, or Lakshmi, while women will relate themselves to a masculine form. A women may see herself as a gopi (cowherd girl from Krishna's boyhood days), pining for Sri Krishna. Roman Catholic nuns marry Jesus.

LIKE A HOMELESS DRUNKARD

Beautiful Mother Kali
My radiant black skinned queen

of the midnight sky!

You stand on your Silent Lover
    like a politician on a soap box
    but your speeches are rivers of love
        and each word becomes a universe

Mother please let me be your roadie
    following you here and there
    carrying your box from town to town

Because I have tasted the intoxicating wine
    of your sweet embrace,
    I am selling my house and everything I own
        and only care to be with you

Having touched your demon-conquering feet,
    I have seen through your eyes
        of unspeakable beauty
          and I have listened through your ears
        of enduring rapture

Now I have fallen madly in love with you
and can only say your name
    Kali Ma! Kali Ma! Kali Ma!
        over and over again
with tears of joy dripping from my chin

I have become an orphan to this world
and, like a homeless drunkard,
    live only for the next cup
        of your all-consuming love

From the book, *Soft Moon Shining*, by Ethan Walker III

THE LEVELS OF DEVOTION

The schools of devotional practice (bhakti yoga) prescribe four levels
at which we may enjoin ourselves in love of the Divine.

1. Puja bhava
2. Stava bhava
3. Dhyana bhava
4. Brahma bhava

Bhava means "attitude" or "mood."

Puja bhava is the mood of ritualistic worship. This can be as simple as offering incense to the Lord, or it can take the form of very complex rituals requiring several hours to complete. In either case, the mood of love is enacted like a play or drama. It is a heartfelt offering to God. Puja bhava should be joyous and deep, dripping like honey with the sweetness of ecstatic communion. These rituals are vehicles for the expression of our love.

Stava bhava is the mood of prayer. This can be a deep, longing prayer in which the seeker pours out his thoughts and feelings to the Beloved, perhaps expressing his or her love with tears streaming down the cheeks. Also, there is prayer which is having a continuous talk with God. We may be asking God for instruction or direction regarding any mundane matter. This continuous dialogue, or, more specifically, unbroken remembrance of God, is what Paul referred to as praying without ceasing (1 Thes. 5:17).

Dhayana bhava is the mood of meditating on God or the contemplation of the beauty, compassion and glory of God. In this mood, one is simply gazing into the eyes of the Beloved, soaring in the presence of cosmic royalty like a seagull hanging in the winds that sweep upward from the cliffs of direct revelation. We are absorbed in the Divine, the mind becomes still, and our prayer beads drop to the floor. Tears of ecstatic joy flood our eyes.

In *Brahma bhava* the "I" merges in the Beloved. Now there is no longer an individual to claim ownership of the ego. The sense of separateness is gone. God has become everything and the doer of all activity, including the very thoughts that may or may not appear on the screen of our minds. There is now only God. Our body is now God's body. God is now the world. We may act, but it is now God acting. We may have thoughts, but it is now God having the thoughts. We delight in the freedom, but it is now God that experiences the delight. There may be an ego, but it now belongs to God – it is now only a mask that God puts on to play a part in His theater of the sublime.

The Total Madness of Her Love

Mother dwells at the center of my being,
forever delightfully at play.
Whatever conditions of consciousness may arise,
I hear through them the music of her life-giving names,
    Om Tara, Om Kali.

Closing my eyes, I perceive the radiant Black Mother
    as indivisible, naked awareness,
dancing fiercely or gently on my heart lotus.
She wears a garland of snow-white skulls,
bright emblem of freedom from birth and death.
Gazing upon her resplendent nakedness,
all concepts and conventions vanish.

Those who judge by mundane standards call me mad.
Timid and limited persons can think what they wish.
My only longing is to express
    the total madness of her love.

This poet child of the Wisdom Goddess
    cries out with abandon:
"The Queen of the Universe
    resides within the flower of my secret heart.
Mother! Mother! Mother!
I seek refuge at your beautiful feet,
delicate and fragrant as the dark blue lotus.
As my body dissolves into earth
    and my mind into space,
may I dissolve into you."
        Ramprasad[8], *Mother of the Universe*, poems of Ramprasad
        translated by Lex Hixon, published by Quest Books.

---

[8] Ramprasad Sen was born in 1723 in Bengal, India. He was a lover of God in the form of the Divine Mother.

THE CONNECTION

It is important that we understand the fundamental nature of our connection to God. Initially, we look within ourselves to find God. The important thing to know is that "within" does not stop at the center of our body. Our inner being is as vast and infinite as outer space. The difference is that as we go within, the forms of existence become increasingly more unified as archetypes or principalities in a hierarchy of consciousness. As we go outward, the forms of existence become more in number, more complex, and more diverse.

The *I-Ching* or *Chinese Book of Changes* illustrates this beautifully. At the center of being is the changeless Tao. This manifests in form as the primal duality of yin and yang. Yang is symbolically represented as a solid line: ——. Yin is represented by a broken line: — —. These two can then be combined in four ways: ⚌ ⚍ ⚎ ⚏.

By adding either a yang line or yin line to each we will have eight archetypes: ☷ ☶ ☵ ☴ ☳ ☲ ☱ ☰.

Each of these transformations is like a layer on an onion continuing ad infinitum. From this, we see how the diversity in the world we perceive with our five senses is generated from only two principalities. Our personalities and bodies are ripples in one or more of the outer skins. But at the core, every being, sentient or insentient, physical or subtle, is exactly the same. Understanding how we are connected to God and to everyone else helps us to have faith that we can realize and enter into our connection with God.

> M: "When one sees God does one see Him with these eyes?"

> Master: "God cannot be seen with these physical eyes. In the course of spiritual discipline one gets a 'love body,' endowed with 'love eyes,' 'love ears,' and so on. One sees God with those 'love eyes.' One hears the voice of God with those 'love ears.' One even gets a sexual organ made of love."

> At these words M. burst out laughing.

The Master continued, unannoyed, "With this 'love body' the soul communes with God."

Ramakrishna, *Gospel of Ramakrishna*, translated by Swami Nikhilananda

Sri Ramakrishna is telling us that we can connect with God and communicate with God directly by developing a "love body." This connection and communion is even more intimate and direct than talking to our spouses or best friends. In the beginning, we may feel little or no connection to God. As the practice of devotion develops and expands, this conduit of communion begins to form between God and ourselves. We discover a long, sealed hatchway in our psyche that we begin to slowly dismantle, thus allowing love to flow from God to us in ever-increasing measures. As this connection develops, we experience feelings of intense bliss, ecstatic joyous weeping, intoxicated laughter, and deep communion.

As our connection expands in frequency and intensity, a subtlety or sensitivity of mind develops. This increased sensitivity, along with inexplicable waves of ecstatic love, leads us to the direct knowledge that these experiences are actually and definitely God returning our love. It will seem as though we had been chipping a hole from the inside of our prison wall of the ego, and God had been chipping a hole from the outside, and then we break through. We continue chipping away through devotional practice and the hole enlarges.

At last it is large enough for us to touch fingers with God. Tears will come easily and frequently. We will say God's name and have tears.[9] Soon, the hole becomes large enough for us to step through and embrace God completely and be embraced by God, personally and directly. We will begin to experience God's love spontaneously and in strange places, such as the grocery store checkout line. When we experience God's love in this way, it is more than simply God throwing blessings on us. It is as direct and personal as if we were talking to another human being. We know we are talking and walking with God, and we know God is also directly aware of us.

_____

[9] The word "tears" is used both literally and as a metaphor indicating the whole of devotional experience.

Eventually, the specific form of God we have chosen to worship becomes the universe and all of its beings as a whole. Oddly, this expansive way of relating to our Beloved becomes the most intimate.

Have You Seen Our Mother Divine?

Brother Wind
Have you seen our Mother?
   Was she sitting alone and silent
   on some lofty snow capped peak
      as you crossed the Rocky Mountains
      on your way to caress
      the vast prairie grasslands?

If you see our most beautiful Mother
   please tell her I am calling her
   and that I love her so very much

Sister Earth
Have you felt our Mother's footsteps
   as she walked across your endless lands
   planting the seeds
      of creation and dissolution?

Have you heard her singing her sweet song
   of compassion and love?
      If so, tell her that her child
      who loves her so very much
         has awakened from his long nap
         and yearns to hug his Mother once again

Sister Ocean
Has our Mother passed through your rivers today
   on her way to direct the waters of eternity
   up into her garden of clouds
      floating in the deep blue sky of primal awareness?

Or have you felt her moving in the unfathomable depths
   of your inky black belly
      where she often goes to stir
      the boiling cauldron of destiny?

If you know where our sweetest of Mothers is
    please tell her
    that I am unable to stop the flood of tears
        that rises from the well of my deep longing
            and that I yearn to hold her
            and to be held by her again

Brother Sun
Nothing at all escapes your warm life-giving gaze!
Please look all around now from your high place
        and tell me if you see our Mother's dancing form
            as she goes about her many tasks
                —can you catch a glimpse of her shadow
                as it plays on the steep cliffs of revelation?

If so, please tell her to come for her child
    who stands now in his crib
        gripping tightly and shaking
        the constraining rail of the ego
            crying Mother! Mother! Mother!
            over and over again
                unable to find contentment in anything but her

If you see her
    please kiss her affectionately for me
    and tell her to come quickly
        as I am through sleeping and dreaming
        and only want to be with her

From the book, *Soft Moon Shining*, by Ethan Walker III

THE EVOLUTION OF DEVOTION

In the beginning we are small, suckling babes. As our practice of love
for God expands, our pride diminishes and is replaced by a dawning
sense of innocence. God begins to feed us the bread of His love.
When a worker honeybee is fed a special substance called "royal
jelly" by the other bees, she is transformed into a queen bee. In the
same way, we are transformed and made pure by this love, this
philosopher's stone, this nectar of immortality. God reveals Himself

as the world and all the beings in it. The suffering of the world is seen as an opportunity to serve God. We are transformed into beings of love and compassion. It is only natural that in the beginning we see our spiritual practice as something that will benefit us. Eventually, this will change, and we will see our practice as something we do with an end to benefiting and serving others and all of life.

CHAPTER 3

The Practice of Love

The path of love has two aspects:
1) The cultivation of love
2) The avoidance of negative tendencies

THE DAILY DOSE OF LOVE

Simply put, our goal is to love God with all of the intensity we can summon. We will discuss two methods of devotional practice. Sitting practice is a formal and regular event, while walking practice is what we do as we walk through the events of our day. With devotional practice there is no single, correct way. Anything that encourages and cultivates our feeling of love for God can be included as part of our practice. We are free to invent or discover our own way to do this. The battlefields of our minds and subconscious realms are littered with the wreckage and carnage of past emotional wounds, blockages, and traumas, and we must find a way to get around or through these obstacles as we journey to the heart. Therefore, what works well for one may not invoke any love at all for another. Each of us will explore those areas of passage in the mind and subconscious that will allow us to travel to the ocean of divine love. At this point, we are not so concerned with stopping to clean the battlefield. Once the garden of love has begun to bloom, love will clean our minds and deep subconscious parts quite spontaneously, with very little consideration from us. There are many paths to the heart, but we only need to find the one that works for us.

In the beginning, we endeavor to find some small crevice into which we can plant our hook. We are finding and establishing the small spark. We can begin with something as simple as a casual interest in God or a mild curiosity. We may consider this to be a feeble position, but it does not take much to start. A roaring bonfire begins by first lighting a few small twigs. We take whatever connection we can make, and we work with it by making an effort to dwell on it. We try to keep our mind focused on it. We try to remember it several times each day. Eventually, mild interest will begin to visit us with fleeting glimpses of Supreme Love. The important ingredients here are patience and persistence.

VISUALIZE LOVE

Love is something we cultivate like a rose garden. We kindle the feeling of love and then direct it toward God. We visualize with our feelings. We can evoke or remember a feeling in the same way that we use our mind's eye to visualize a tree or any other object. In this case we are using the "heart's eye."

To illustrate, we might close our eyes and try to feel a gamut of emotions: peace, joy, or sadness. This is what we mean by visualizing feelings. Instead of *seeing* something, we *feel* something. In this way, we begin to see how we are going to develop love for God. We will mentally visualize God in the form with which we are most comfortable and then "visualize," with our feelings, our flow of love toward our Beloved. We will also visualize the feeling of God's love coming back to us. The form of God matters little. Our affections can just as easily be directed to an incarnation of God such as Jesus, Buddha, or Krishna.

Because love has slipped away from most of us, there are some useful exercises for rekindling the feeling of love – getting the spark going. When we were children, perhaps we had a puppy or a kitty that we loved very much. We can try to remember what that love felt like, and eventually we will recall the feeling. Maybe we loved our mother or perhaps a special grandma or grandpa. We can try to remember what that love felt like.

The ability to bring forth the feeling of love may be strenuous at first. Also, our best effort may yield only a tiny spark. With practice this will grow in much the same way that lifting weights will cause our physical muscles to grow. With constant practice, the small, barely perceptible spark of love will become a flame, then a blaze, and then a roaring bonfire of divine love-light.

The Bonfire of Single Minded Devotion

Beloved Mother of all beings
I am abandoning this mind
  like so many sticks of wood
  thrown into a large pile
    on the vast field of your Divine Love

Joyously we strike the match of devotion
  and set it to this wooden pile of ancient habits
    that now lies motionless and broken

Flames grow quickly and spread about the base
  and then begin to roar
  as the bonfire of single minded devotion
    leaps into the night sky
      sending sparks of joyous dissolution
      into upward swirling spirals

And as the last ember flickers
  into the void of unrestrained existence
    we stop our dance of divine madness
    which had moved us in the ecstasy of surrender
    around and around the burning fire

Sitting, at last, alone and together
  we enjoy the silence of the stars

From the book, *Soft Moon Shining*, by Ethan Walker III

Feeling Innocent

As our practice of love progresses, we will begin to experience an increased awareness or feeling of our own innocence, especially during periods of intense communion. When innocence comes, we have the opportunity to pay close attention to it. We can try to grab hold of it, like a shipwreck survivor swimming in the water who happens upon a drifting lifeboat. This feeling of innocence is a powerful salve that we can apply to our many mental and emotional afflictions, such as pride, shame, jealousy, and anger. The taste of innocence is so sweet and light. Innocence feels so good, and parlays into a striking contrast with the staggering weight of our darkly ponderous ego. As a meditation, we can swim in the clear waters of innocence and that will further enhance our ability to love God. Having connected with our innocence, we can call it forth at any time by simply remembering the feeling and keeping the mind focused on it with the intensity of a cat watching a mouse.

Devotional practice delivers us into the arms of innocence, regardless of what errors we may have committed in the past. As we become more familiar, more identified with the fire of devotion that now begins to surge and roar in our hearts, we accept our many character defects and simply resolve to work on them. We understand that at the core we are innocent and, in fact, we share that innocence with every human being, no matter what they may or may not have done in the past. Our identification with our faults begins to diminish. We begin to become emotionally self-sufficient.

INNOCENT CHILD

In the deep of the night when my mind is fast asleep
I will slip out to meet you
  in the open field that lays
  like a fallow earthen pool collecting stardust.

When the coming and the going is fast asleep
  I will run with open arms
    like an eagle soaring in the wind of your breath
      eager to embrace you.

When the dance of my small desires slumbers
  I will water this blooming life
  with the river of tears
    that pours from my deep longing
      for the vision of your innocent child.

From the book, Soft Moon Shining, by Ethan Walker III

SITTING PRACTICE

In the beginning, it is very important to maintain a consistent daily time and place for practicing love for God. Otherwise, our minds will be too distracted to remember to practice. This can be once or twice a day. Having our communion with God at a regular time and place helps to overcome that aspect of our mind that is lazy and inert. We can call this "couch potato mind."

It is good if we can resolve to sit for a certain period of time. It is important to carefully and thoughtfully select an amount of time that we can consistently follow day after day. In our newly appointed eagerness, we may bite off more than we can chew. When the initial infatuation wears off, we must be able to sustain our daily effort by pure grit and determination alone. After some time, our effort will begin to bear fruit and we will begin to find sustenance in drinking from the spring of devotion, our newfound oasis of love. Prior to finding our oasis, there is the initial trek across the desert, and we must pace ourselves to make the journey. As we become more absorbed in the ocean of love, our sitting time will increase gradually and naturally, without any effort on our part.

It is helpful to have a personal alter, shrine, or chapel that is devoted to our Beloved. It can be small, taking up no more space than the corner of our bedroom. How the alter is appointed is a personal matter, but typically it is populated with pictures, icons, and statues as well as items we can offer each day such as burning candles and incense. Small amounts of a food item or a cup of tea can be brought with us as a gift for our Beloved when we come to sit at the altar. It is not that any of these items in themselves should be deemed as ritualistically absolute, but rather they are simply used to direct feelings of love to God. Anything at all that serves to enhance our personal love for God is useful for our practice.

If we are able to visualize the complete form of our Beloved, then we can sit with eyes closed and invent ways to interact. If we are not able to see the whole form clearly, we can visualize a part like the hand or the face, or try to feel that we are touching or being held by our Beloved. As another example, we might want to imagine that we are dancing hand in hand or that we are sitting in front of our Beloved, offering candy from our heart, and placing it in God's mouth. We see our Beloved eating the candy with great joy. Each time we offer the candy we express our love.

Most importantly, we practice feeling love. That is the important thing. The activities and interactions are only for this – feeling love. We might imagine we are a little child climbing onto God's lap and as we put our small arms and hands around God's neck, we whisper softly, "I love you so very much."

We might try to feel God's love and presence coming up from inside the depths of our being much like peering into a deep, dark well, and singing extemporaneous songs expressing our admiration for God's beauty, compassion, and other qualities. We call God to come and play with us. If we are able to feel love for God as we do this, God will not be able to refuse. If we are unable to visualize anything, then we can work with our eyes open. With a picture or statue of our Beloved in front of us, we can enact the same dance of love.

If we have a mantra or prayer for our Beloved, we can try to say each round with love. A supplication might be inserted in between each round such as, "I love you because you are so compassionate. I love you because you are so beautiful. I want only to be with you." This helps to keep the feeling of love active so that the saying of the mantra does not fall into a mechanical rut.

If we are alone, we can try dramatizing the saying of our mantra, prayer, or extemporaneous supplications as if we were a suitor in an Italian opera, standing in the courtyard, singing to the one who has captured our hearts. Repeatedly we throw our arms into the air with great passion, as if reaching out to God. Our yearning and love for God soaks into the marrow of our bones and we are carried away like stardust in a divine wind. If we have trouble feeling this, acting as though we feel it will encourage the feeling. We act it out until the feeling comes. Fake it until you make it.

WALKING PRACTICE

In addition to our first line of practice, our daily devotional sitting, we can also engage our hearts in the love of God during the day.

This is important because we want our love for God to become a way of life and not a unique activity that happens once or twice a day. As before, we are left to invent our own methods and construct our own tools.

The drive to work is a good space for this. We can try to see our Beloved as manifesting in the clouds and sky or any other natural beauty. Seeing this, we can call to God, sing to God, or pray to God. We might inwardly vow to do these practices for 10 minutes, which could be the distance from our driveway to 42nd Street. Then we can play the radio. In time, the duration of our practice will increase naturally.

If we are fond of repeating a mantra, God's name, or a prayer like the *Our Father*, a digital cooking timer can be very useful to keep the mind on track. Set the timer for 1 minute or more, and as it beeps at the end of the time, use it as a reminder to say the mantra or prayer. Then hit the reset and start button to begin the cycle again. If the mind wanders, the timer serves as a reminder to apply ourselves with love and mindfulness.

If we work at a computer, we can set our daily reoccurring event scheduler to remind us twice a day to stop for 30 seconds and love God. A wristwatch that beeps on the hour can be another cue to remember our Beloved. We can pray before meals or make a resolve to talk to God while we are brushing our teeth.

Any event which occurs regularly in our day can be set, with a little effort, to remind us to love God. Sitting alone in a chair while waiting to see someone can be an opportunity to talk to God. We can consult with God concerning mundane decisions, as well as play with God and joke with Him. God is like a good-natured puppy dog ready to play tug with any old rag we might have at hand.

Another useful tack is to offer things to God – something dear to us. For example, we might give up chocolate for one day as a gift to God, or we can give it up for a week or for the rest of our life. We can vow to say a certain prayer to God so many times a day for a period of time. We are free to find anything to give to God as an expression of our love.

A Country Fair for Those Mad with Love

Drive me out of my mind, O Mother!
What use is esoteric knowledge
   or philosophical discrimination?
Transport me totally with the burning wine
   of your all-embracing love.

Mother of Mystery, who imbues with mystery
   the hearts of those who love you,
   immerse me irretrievably
   in the stormy ocean without boundary,
   pure love, pure love, pure love.

Wherever your lovers reside
   appears like a madhouse
   to common perception.
Some are laughing with your freedom,
   others weep tears of your tenderness,
   still others dance, whirling with your bliss.
Even your devoted Gautama, Moses,
   Krishna, Jesus, Nanak, and Muhammad
   are lost in the rapture of pure love.

This poet stammers,
   overcome with longing:
"When? When? When?
When will I be granted companionship
   with her intense lovers?"
Their holy company is heavenly,
   a country fair for those mad with love,
   where every distinction
   between master and disciple
      disappears.

This lover of love sings:
Mother! Mother! Mother!
Who can fathom your mystery,
   your eternal play of love with love?
You are divine madness, O Goddess,
   your love the brilliant crown of madness.

Please make this poor poet madly wealthy
with the infinite treasure of your love."

Ramprasad, *Mother of the Universe*, poems of Ramprasad
translated by Lex Hixon, published by Quest Books.

CRYING TO GOD

Ammachi frequently mentions crying to God. In the practice of devotion and love, crying to God is the goal in terms of that which is
outwardly visible. In fact, she states directly and clearly that if one
gets tears for God, one is saved (read *Saved by a Few Tears* in the
section *Useful Instruction from Ammachi*). In her dialogues, we see
her repeatedly begging and pleading with those around her to cry for
God. It is in this state that the heart opens completely, and God's
grace pours into us like a rainstorm in the desert causing long-dor-
mant divine flowers to bloom. We become innocent like little children. Our cup of joy overflows. The heavy burden of delusional
self-importance is washed away in the torrential rain of love, and we
find ourselves floating in the indescribable lightness of being like a
cloud in the deep blue sky. We feel that we belong to all of life. We
feel loved. We are radiant with love for everyone and everything. We
are consumed in the ecstasy and bliss of our mystical union with God.
As the flood subsides, peace comes easily and completely, shining like
the full autumn moon rising on the horizon of love's bountiful harvest.

Crying for God can take two forms. One is born from the longing for
God. The intensity of our longing and subsequent pain of separation
brings these tears. This happens during periods of concentration on
our feeling of being incomplete, wanting answers, and needing to be
loved. The other form of crying happens when we make contact with
God. These tears flow from the intensity of gratitude and joy that God
has connected with us, and also from feeling pure flowing love for our
Beloved. We feel that we are bursting with so much love we are not
able to contain the rush of it and the overflow comes out in tears.

At first most of us will not feel like crying. There are several things
we can do. The first is our meditating on God and visualizing the
feeling of love toward God. This will gradually loosen the hard
shell around our heart and cause it to open. The second is to pray to

God to help us have tears of love. The third is to attempt to induce a cry while thinking of God. Children can work up a cry, but we have forgotten how. At first we might describe these beginnings as base emotionalism, but that is perfectly all right. All spiritual practices begin with a dualistic bent that later purifies and evolves into a deeper aspect. Working ourselves into a cry for God by any means of concentration and mental gymnastics is perfectly acceptable. This will eventually evolve into pure love for God. If we are not able to cry, we can pray whole-heartedly and sincerely, with as much intensity as possible. All of this creates the head of steam necessary to cause the ego to break down and the heart to open.

At first we may get a little moistening of the eyes, but not too frequently. With practice, this turns into dripping tears of joy, and it happens more often. We will eventually be able to slip easily into communion with the Lord and the resulting flood of tears, by simply saying the name of our Beloved with a little concentration. It will also begin to happen spontaneously and sometimes in awkward circumstances. We may be in the grocery store checkout line, and something the checker does will remind us of our Beloved, and we will be overwhelmed with love and wet eyes. We will be compelled to mumble something about allergies as we wipe away the moisture with our shirtsleeve.

Eventually, all of this will culminate in the sense or "knowing" that we know God personally and directly, in the same way that we know any person with whom we are aquainted. We will also know, beyond all doubt, that God is equally aware of us in a very intimate and personal way. As we contemplate this newly revealed reality, and as we continue our practice of enjoining ourselves to pure love for God, and as the tears flow, our minds and hearts will purify.

This brings us around to the baseline task of eliminating the ego. We will begin to clearly see the ego as the spoiler of our love and communion. As a result, we will beg God to remove it. Now, we are both pulling toward God and pushing away from the ego. The pushing and pulling is amplified and intensified. Like antiwar protestors in the 60s, our thoughts will continuously parade through our mind with placards like, "Get us out of the ego now," or "Heck no, we won't ego!" This is the pushing away from the old, delusional way of seeing. The pulling is our intensified love for God and the resulting communion. We begin to feel that our previously cherished pleasures of the world are tasteless sawdust compared with the joy and the delight of the divine. Crying tears for God is the expression of this beautiful cosmic dance of liberation.

Weepers of the World

Salvation awaits the weepers of the world
   who shed shimmering pools of tears
      longing for the Divine.

Blessed are they that cry for God
   For She will surely come
      as a mother who will not fail
         to cuddle her crying child.

And if the pump handle of devotion
   brings only empty hollow clanks
      from beneath the ground of our heart
         then we must fall on our knees and weep
            that tears have failed to roll down our cheeks
         and if those tears also fail
            we must dust our eyes with pepper
               as an act of sheer desperation.

Pray to our Divine Mother
   that she deliver us
      from the dry barren desert
         of the intellect.

And carry us into the verdant garden
   of Divine Love
      from which we may eat
         of the sweet fruit of immortal bliss.

       From the book, *Soft Moon Shining*, by Ethan Walker III

Note: The author refers to dusting the eyes with pepper figuratively and does not suggest this should actually be attempted.

SINGING TO GOD

All of a sudden the Holy Mother closed Her eyes and sat motionless, Her face lit with a blissful smile. All the devotees who were gathered around Her began meditating. A couple of minutes passed and when Mother slowly opened Her eyes She began rapturously singing.

By which Power this world had been created,
By which Power it is sustained,
By which Power does it return to the unmanifest state,
Let us offer our salutations to that Great Power...

Everyone joined Her and went into an ecstatic mood. The Holy Mother shed tears of bliss, now and then calling out, "Amma, Amma" while continuing the singing. Her poignant song and elevated spiritual mood filled the devotees' hearts with tremendous peace and tranquility. Forgetting the world around them, they sang with great devotion.
Swami Amritaswarupananda, *Awaken Children*, vol. I, p. 32

Singing to God is a powerful means of opening the floodgates of love for God. We should pour every fiber of our being into the singing of these songs, imagining our Beloved as the words and melodies tumble from our lips. Unfurling our pure white sails of deep longing, we are swept away in the cosmic winds of God's unfolding grace.

AMAZING GRACE

Amazing Grace
How sweet the sound
To save a wretch like me

I once was lost
But now I'm found;
Was blind, but now I see.

John Newton 1725-1807.
Mr. Newton was a slave trader before coming to Jesus.

The Blessing of a Great Soul

The most direct path to the wellspring of devotion is to be "touched" by a soul who is permanently absorbed in the Divine. Before matches were invented, fires were kept burning continuously in the homes of villagers. If someone's fire went out for some reason, then one of the children was sent nextdoor with a small container designed to get a flame. The flame was thus passed from one house to another as needed. In the same way, awakened souls carry a limitless supply of divine matches, which they are ready to strike and apply to their hearts. However, these great ones, in their wisdom, will be able to see if their hearts have reached the point of combustibility. Sincere love and innocent longing are the dry twigs and tinder that great souls look for. Humility and childlike innocence are the sure path to receiving the grace of these divine souls.

> Amma: A real Guru is one who is endowed with all the Divine qualities, such as equal vision, universal love, renunciation, compassion, patience, forbearance, and endurance. He will have complete control over his mind. He will be like a huge ship which can carry thousands of passengers. His mere presence will give a feeling of protection and safety, an assurance to the disciple that he will reach the goal. Like the moon his presence will be cooling, soothing and heart-capturing, but at the same time it will also be brilliant, radiant and shining like the sun. He will be soft like a flower and hard like a diamond in his manner towards the disciple. He will be simpler than the simplest and humbler than the humblest. Even his silence will be a teaching. A real disciple is one who can imbibe the life and teachings of such a Guru and follow his footsteps faithfully. Knowing and understanding the real nature of such a Great Master, a true disciple's heart will spontaneously surrender and willingly let him discipline him.

> It is not possible to proceed very far on the spiritual path without a Guru. A guide is necessary to travel in an undiscovered country. A sadhak, through his penances, may succeed in getting rid of his gross vasanas without the help of a Perfect Master, but a Satguru's help and Grace are a must in

order to eliminate the subtle vasanas and to give up his individuality. There is a son who comes here. One day he openly told one of the brahmacharins that he had been doing spiritual practices for the last thirty-five years but never had a deep experience. He also said that he knows his problem which he stated was nothing but the hesitancy to come under the discipline of a Satguru. His subtle vasanas still remained even after thirty-five years of severe penance. He is a very sincere and hard-working son, yet no real experience occurred. This is what happens to people who cannot surrender. Once you come under a Perfect Master, then you simply obey his words and do sadhana without fail. If your surrender is complete and if you are determined to attain the goal, he will work with your ego, both the gross and subtle, and will take you across the ocean of transmigration. The subtle ego is very hard to break through with only your own efforts. The Satguru's guidance will slowly bring it out and exhaust it. A Perfect Master always works with the ego of the disciple. But he will not start until the disciple is ready for it.

Mother does not want to insist that anyone do this. I f it is the Lord's will that someone should be here, let it be so. If it is to be that one should be somewhere else, let that be so. Sadhana will become smoother and easier if a Satguru is present.

Ammachi, *Awaken Children*, vol. III, p. 173

PITFALLS ON THE PATH OF DEVOTION

NEGATIVE THOUGHTS

This section on negative thoughts will help us gain a clearer understanding of how negative thoughts operate in the mind, that they all have the I-thought as their root, and that they are all the opposite of love.

When the fire of our love begins to burn brightly enough, negative thoughts will be consumed automatically.

Let no debt remain outstanding, except the continuing debt to love one another, for he who loves his fellowman has fulfilled the law. The commandments, "Do not commit adultery," "Do not murder," "Do not steal," "Do not covet," and whatever other commandment there may be, are summed up in this one rule: "Love your neighbor as yourself." Love does no harm to its neighbor. Therefore love is the fulfillment of the law. Romans 13:8-10, NIV

However, until we reach the point of combustion, it will be important for us to make an effort to recognize and remove negative thinking. Negative thoughts and emotions cause the light and love in the heart to recoil and retreat, like a crawdad that has just been poked with a stick. When these negatives occupy our mind, God will be far away. They are like holes in the cauldron of our devotion that cause our love to leak away. Thus, it becomes difficult to make progress, because we cannot contain enough intensity in our love and devotion. We are constantly distracted by these afflictions. They make the heart hard, small, and dark. Love simply cannot exist in the atmosphere of these negative tendencies, in the same way that grass will not grow under a rock. Negative emotions are caused by our desires for the objects of our senses – persons, places, and things. We refer to the presence of these desires as worldliness.

The mind soaked in worldliness may be compared to a wet match-stick. You won't get a spark, however much you may rub it. Sri Ramakrishna, *The Gospel of Sri Ramakrishna*, p. 242

Question: Is it possible to know God for those of us who are ordinary people?

Mother: Children, God is also ordinary at all times and therefore not difficult to know. But there is one thing. The ignorant ones who are drowning themselves in worldliness cannot know the Truth. Whoever it may be, he who has sincere interest can know and see God.

Ammachi, *Awaken Children*, vol. 1, p. 37

Do not love the world or anything in the world. If anyone loves the world, the love of the Father is not in him. For everything in the world—the cravings of sinful man, the lust of his eyes and the boasting of what he has and does—comes not from the Father but from the world. The world and its

desires pass away, but the man who does the will of God
lives forever.   1 John 2:15-17, NIV

"Meaningless! Meaningless!" says the Teacher. "Utterly
meaningless! Everything is meaningless."
                                          Ecclesiastes 1:2, NIV

I have seen all the things that are done under the sun; all of
them are meaningless, a chasing after the wind.
                                         Ecclesiastes 1:14, NIV

These scriptures advise us to see all worldly endeavors that are con-
scripted for our own pleasure or indulgence as meaningless. In contrast, the only meaningful personal human pursuit is love, and the
only meaningful relationship to the world is to express compassion
and relieve the suffering of others. If we move away from worldliness, we will move away from negative emotions.

If we look closely at these spoilers of happiness, we will find that
they are all dependent on the I-thought for their existence. They are
the fruit of the ego. It is the I-thought that gives rise to its lieuten-
ants who are:

1. Desire
2. Anger
3. Greed
4. Jealousy
5. Attachment
6. Pride

Only in our sense of separation and aloneness–in the absence of
love–can these afflictions take root and grow, like a fungus that
grows only in dark places. Their presence fortifies the illusion of
being a separate ego by granting the ego an imagined substance or
reality. It becomes a vicious downward spiral. For example, the ego
is angry with someone else. If the I-thought is the root, the trunk is
"Who am I?" The branches are "I am angry" and the leaves are "I
am angry at him or her or it." The ego is then satisfied that all of
this "makes me who I am." The ego establishes these relationships,
for good or ill, to define itself. It has an existence that is only rela-
tive to other persons or objects. Like a mirror, the ego has no sub-

stance of its own but is simply the reflection of many contrived relationships and definitions. God is love, and these negative thoughts and feelings are anti-love.

Desire

Desire is the "want" for what we don't have. This can be desire for personal relationships, a place (the grass is always greener), or objective things like cars and money, control of others, status, and pleasure. Lust and gluttony also fall into the category of desire. Desire cultivates a self-centered "I"-based reality that, by nature, excludes love. The nature of love is to be oriented toward someone other than ourselves. Thus, self-serving desires do not arise. Desire for the happiness and well-being of others is divine. The difference lies in understanding for whom the bell of desire tolls – our own self-interest or others.

Anger

Anger is related to both desire and attachment. When we fail to satisfy a desire, we are angry. If someone insults us, we are angry because we have a desire to be important and respected. Fear, which is the twin of anger, is the anticipation that we might fail to satisfy a desire. Hatred is a form of anger. Fear of death anticipates the end of the body, for which we have a primal desire. We also desire many things such as food, sex, relationships, travel, and movies, that require a body to enjoy. Most of us have deep-seated anger and fear to some degree or another. Many of these habitual fears and angers were established so long ago that we can't remember why. Anger, fear and hatred have their existence in the I-thought. Love sees another as a Beloved, and this cultivates tolerance and patience thus extinguishing any sparks of anger that might seek a foothold in the mind.

Greed

In our delusional "I"-based reality, we have established the idea that certain things grant us happiness. This causes us to crave and covet them. They are seen as an avenue to pleasure, comfort and security. Of course, this thinking conditions the mind to perceive reality as me, me, me. The obsession with possessing the objects of our desires, we call "greed." We want ours and everybody else's too. Greed drives us like cattle into the canyon of no-love and separateness. In contrast, sharing and giving are symptoms of love and reveal our unity or connectedness.

JEALOUSY

Jealousy is like greed but most often applies to persons. We do not want to share another person with anyone or anything else. For example, we may be jealous if the other person takes up a hobby. As with the other afflictive emotions, jealousy is firmly rooted in the prison of the I-thought and chokes out the tender shoots of love. Love only wants what is best for the other person even if it requires personal sacrifice.

ATTACHMENT

Attachment is different from desire. Attachment is the unwillingness to part with what we now have, and it is also the unwillingness to accept what we don't want. Attachment also applies to concepts, identities and beliefs, while greed has more to do with objects. Clinging and aversion are both forms of attachment. Attachment is like standing in a river and refusing to accept the water that is rushing toward us from upstream and refusing to let go of the water that is rushing away from us in its journey downstream. The events of life are a river, and most of us approach them with the disease of attachment. Such a futile endeavor guarantees that we will be miserable.

The spiritual ideal of detachment bears some further discussion due to the confusion that often accompanies it. When most of us first hear of "attaining detachment," images of being aloof or withdrawn come to mind. We picture ourselves living in a cave high in the Himalayas, subsisting on grass and rainwater. In fact, detachment means the opposite. Detachment means that, as we stand in the river of life, we accept what comes to us and we let go of that which is passing on. This allows us to embrace life; to join life; to say "yes" to all of life. A person who is attached is the one who is avoiding life. This is the one who is aloof. An attached person is rejecting and clinging, and these are both denials of life. It is a denial of what life brings us and a denial of what life takes away.

PRIDE

It has been said that humility is the greatest of virtues. We have also heard that pride comes before a fall. Like the other afflictive emotions, pride separates us from God and others. We are taught to "take pride in our work." We imagine a world without pride to be a world of lazy people living in filth and chaos. With regard to this, we may substitute love for pride and do quite well. We can love our work and offer it to God with love. We can love to do it well, as to make it a good offering. We clean our house because we feel it belongs to God and, out of love, we want to be good caretakers. The difference between actions performed out of love and actions performed out of pride is that love actions are done for someone else, and prideful actions are done to satisfy our own selfish ends. Pride says, "I did it–look at me." Love says, "This is for you."

Pride is exaggerated self-importance. In reality, we are not the body nor even the mind, but part of a Whole. Pride is ignorance of this "belonging." In truth, the Whole is important and not just our own small existence. Therefore, love adheres to this truth by placing importance on God, others, and the Whole, while pride places importance on our small, limited, ego-centered existence.

If someone insults us, our feelings are hurt because the insult shatters our self-importance. If we do not have this self-importance, the insult passes through us. We are not affected by it. This is the power of humility. The lowly grass bends and is not broken when the hurricane blows. Self-pity and self-justification are both forms of pride. Self-pity says, "Poor me" and the sense of being a victim is pronounced by an underlying sense of self-importance. The ego says, "I am very important, and that makes these crimes against me (imagined or otherwise) especially heinous – poor me." As the ego becomes more identified with being a victim, it begins to imagine crimes against it in order to continue the identity. On the other side of self-pity, self-justification says, "I am great." It is the reverse of self-pity. In this case the ego refuses to acknowledge any mistakes or character defects, and sets about constructing meticulous justifications and rationalizations to maintain the delusion of being important.

As part of our devotional practice, it behooves us to develop the habit of watching the mind and its thoughts for the occurrence of any of these love killers. When one of them is noticed, we should jump up and down, stamp our feet, flail our arms, and shout and scream for our Beloved to come and remove the negative thought or feeling. It is the intensity of our calling that counts.

STEERING OUR SHIP

As a man thinketh, so he is. The mind is like a piece of white cloth that takes on the color of whatever is spilled on it. We should consider avoiding situations, places, and people that promote negative emotions in the same way that a recovering alcoholic must stay out of bars. By the same token, it is good to keep the company of persons who are also trying to know God, and it is especially good to keep the company of saints. If we are not able to visit live saints, we can read about them. We can even watch videos about many of them.

Some may contend that the effort to abide in spirituality and avoid negativity is also a form of attachment. This is discrimination and not attachment. The difference is that discrimination perceives the difference between illusion and reality while attachment engages the illusion. Discrimination requires introspection and discernment while attachment is blind and habitual.

In summary, negative thoughts are the "suffering" of our existence. The good news is that we have the power to ignore them. This requires courage, because our ego has invested its identity in these negative points of view. Where there is negativity, love will wither and die. We should not be discouraged if we are not able to stop all detrimental activities at once. We must be patient with ourselves.

LOVING OTHER PEOPLE

The devotee, or lover of God, eventually comes to see the world and everyone in it as God; herein lies the foundation for loving other people. Saying this is easy. However, our goal is to feel it, and that is not so easy. When we love and serve other people, we are loving and serving God directly. The same will apply to animals and Mother Nature.

In a way, it is easier to love other people than it is to love God, because other people are specifically tangible. God is tangible but not specifically as this or that. Rather, God is the entire universe; the universe is God's incarnation. In another way, it is easier to love God than to love other people because of the deep wounds and hurts that we feel we have received from them. We have so much mistrust and sorrowful baggage that it is difficult to tear down our fortress of defense, thus allowing the river of love to flow to others even for a moment. We can rightly feel that God loves us unconditionally as a mother would. God is willing to accept us no matter what sin or crime we might have committed in the past. Because of this, most of us will begin the path of love by loving God, which will then open our hearts enough to begin to love other people. Loving and serving other people is truly loving and serving God.

> When the Son of Man comes in his glory, and all the angels with him, he will sit on his throne in heavenly glory. All the nations will be gathered before him, and he will separate the people one from another as a shepherd separates the sheep from the goats. He will put the sheep on his right and the goats on his left. Then the King will say to those on his right, "Come, you who are blessed by my Father; take your inheritance, the kingdom prepared for you since the creation of the world. For I was hungry and you gave me something to eat, I was thirsty and you gave me something to drink, I was a stranger and you invited me in, I needed clothes and you clothed me, I was sick and you looked after me, I was in prison and you came to visit me." Then the righteous will answer him, "Lord, when did we see you hungry and feed you, or thirsty and give you something to drink? When did we see you a stranger and invite you in, or needing clothes and clothe you? When did we see you sick or in prison and go to visit you?" The King will reply, "I tell you the truth, whatever you did for one of the least of these brothers of mine, you did for me." Matthew 25:31-40 NIV

We should pause to consider that loving other people does not always mean letting them have their own way. A criminal should be imprisoned, not because we must extract punishment as an eye for an eye and a tooth for a tooth; not out of revenge, but as an act of compassion. We save the criminal from himself, and we do not give him the opportunity to continue harming others. Also, and just as important, we must protect society as a whole from his willingness to commit misdeeds. It is our motive that is important.

> Young leader: But Mother, there is a problem when we talk about selflessness. Suppose some aggressors forcefully pluck coconuts from the coconut trees of the ashram and take them away. Now, what would Mother do? Would you simply allow them to take the coconuts or would you call the police? It is selfishness if you call the police, isn't it?
>
> Mother: There is one thing. Everything is one Self. But a dog should be seen as a dog and treated accordingly. Holding a stick against it as if to strike doesn't fall under selfishness. There is no fault in driving away an ignorant dog when it comes to harm us. Mother does not say that this is selfish. There is nothing against selfless action in obstructing a person who does things out of ignorance. Not only that. If he is not prevented, he will become a public nuisance and will create many problems in the society. What is important is that when you punish him, it should be done with a pure intention, that is, to correct him for his future good. It should not be done out of dislike or revenge. One shouldn't act desirous of selfish ends. It is beneficial for the world if you help to punish an aggressor who forcefully climbs on somebody's coconut tree. There the stress is not on selfishness but Dharma.
>
> Ammachi, *Awaken Children*, vol. I, p. 283

How to Forgive

In order to love we must learn how to forgive. For a saint, and for God, forgiving is effortless and natural. For the rest of us it is a profound act of courage, because the ego must die a little each time we forgive. When our lover rejects us, or a childhood classmate tells us we are ugly, or our boss screams at us, our self-importance is damaged. The ego fights to maintain its delusional reality, and it will deploy many defensive maneuvers to counter the attack. Over the span of our life these defenses become so habitual and ingrained that we are not aware of them. When confronted with the opportunity to forgive, we are faced with fear and other defenses, such as anger, stacked one on the other like layers of an onion. Fear will always be at the core. This stems from the ego's primal fear of non-existence. Forgiving the transgressions of others requires that we conquer our fear and allow the ego to step a little closer to the edge of obscurity.

> We are trying to learn how to see God, or the Pure Essence, in everything and everybody and not the demon in them, even in the wicked. If you see the demon in others, the very same negative forces will swallow you up and you yourself will become a demon in the end. Children, that is not our way. Hate evil, not the evil-doer. If somebody is egotistic or selfish, hate egotism or selfishness, not the person. We can do this if we really try. If the son is a drunkard or a drug-addict, the parents will hate his drinking habit or his addiction to drugs but they will still love their son. In fact, such children are often especially loved by the parents. In the same way, try to love others, even if they are bad. The right attitude is, right understanding of a particular situation in life, using proper discrimination, and then wisely putting it into application. Ammachi, *Awaken Children*, vol. III, p. 44

FORGIVING OURSELVES

Forgiving ourselves is necessary if we are going to learn to forgive others. To some degree, most of us are stricken with a sense of shame and unworthiness. These are delusional characteristics of the ego, and they prevent us from feeling close to God and also to others. Shame is a large obstacle, and we will want to make an effort to remove it. To overcome shame, we learn to accept ourselves just as we are, including our "sordid past" and our negative traits. The past is dead and gone like so much dust in the wind and lives only as a phantom in our minds.

Accepting our faults does not mean we are giving them a permanent home in our minds. We simply say to ourselves, "Okay, this is where I am. I accept myself as is. I have these bad habits and I fully recognize them. From this day on I am setting a course to eliminate the bad things in my character. If others do not like me because I am not perfect, then I accept that." This is a conversation we will have with our mind many times in order to talk it down out of its madness. We replace the old habit of shame and self-deprecation with one of acceptance, followed with a sense of resolve to do right. If we happen to fall down in our effort to remove our demons, we get up and try again. As the saying goes, the only failure is giving up.

Now that we have accepted ourselves "as is," we fearlessly pursue the process of cataloging and accepting our faults with the ultimate goal of eliminating them. It is not possible to eliminate a fault if we do not acknowledge that we have it. It is not possible to accept ourselves if we do not acknowledge these faults. When faced with another person pointing out a fault to us, our responses slowly become more liberated. Instead of fuming or taking a swing at the person, we are able to reply, "Yes, I am covetous like that at times. You are right. I'm working on it." We are not defensive because we accept ourselves and we are secure in our own acceptance. We no longer require the approval of others (relativistic ego thinking) to feel that we are all right.

As our acceptance takes root, we begin to see clearly that everyone else has a set of stories to tell. Their stepfathers beat them, others rejected them in high school, their mothers were alcoholics, and other soul-stifling scenarios. We begin to kindle a spirit of forgiveness and tolerance for the transgressions of others. We understand that everyone is trying to do the best they can with what they have. The problem is that we are all somewhat mad with our delusions. How is it possible to grow up in this world with its emphasis on self-centered addictions, pleasure at any cost, and unbridled pursuit of sensual gratification through things and manipulation of others, and not be a "work of chaos?"

We can apply this acceptance of others and ourselves like a new-found magic potion. Anytime we are with other people, at home, at work, while walking in the mall, we practice – we rub the balm on our minds. We look at the people and remind ourselves that they too inherited a bag full of worms from the point of their very birth. We accept them as they are, and we resolve to do what we can to relieve their suffering instead of adding to it. Wherever two or more are gathered, we practice seeing others in this light.

Original Innocence

Original innocence is another antidote that we can apply to our unforgiving minds. This is the understanding that at the core of every human being there is only innocence. If, in the beginning, there was only God, then everything that exists can only be made from God. This means it is not possible for anyone or anything to exist outside of God or apart from God. So much for rational arguments.

This spaghetti will not stick to the wall unless we try to experience the innocence for ourselves by finding innocence within ourselves. We can reflect on our childhood and try to recapture the spirit of being an innocent child. As mentioned earlier in this book, the practice of devotion will facilitate this. If we can get so much as a glimpse of our inherent innocence, we will simultaneously see an innocent child within every other human being, without exception. With this knowledge in hand, we can begin to apply it to the mind's habitual tendency to project its own blame and shame onto others. This causes a fundamental shift in how we understand and communicate with others. Instead of being judgmental, which is an outgoing act of projecting our own neuroses onto others, we become receptive. We understand each person, even though he or she may behave poorly. This is the ability to "receive" the other person, no matter what. This in turn opens our hearts and permits our love to flow to them.

> "Amma, what do you mean by receptivity? How can one be receptive?" asked a devotee.

> "Receptivity comes where there is love within," Amma answered. "Love helps you to be open, open like a child. Love makes you innocent like a child. A child is the most receptive person. Receptivity is the power to believe, the power to have faith, the ability to accept love. It is the

power to prevent doubt from entering your mind. Receptivity is the ability to accept all experiences of life without reacting to them.

"Receptivity makes you simple. A receptive person is like an innocent child. If you want to be closer to God, try to be like a child. A child's world is full of wonder and imagination and play. As you get older this look of wonder disappears from your eyes. You cannot play anymore. You cannot believe anymore; like so many grown-ups, you can only doubt.

"Have you watched children play? They can imagine that a small sand heap is a big castle. At one moment white sand is sugar for them, and the next moment it is salt. A rope with its ends tied together becomes a car or a bus. For them a rock can be a throne, and a leaf becomes a big fan. Sometimes they imagine that a long coconut frond is a serpent. They can believe in anything. If you tell a child that rain is the water that falls down when the celestial beings who live in the sky wash their dishes, he will believe you; a child won't express any doubt. This openness, the power to accept, is receptivity. Don't think that Amma is asking you to believe in everything people tell you. She is only asking you to have faith in the Satguru's words, and in the words of the great saints and sages who have realized and experienced the ultimate goal of life.

"As we get older, we lose all enthusiasm and joy. We become dry and unhappy. Why? Because we lose our faith and innocence. It is good for you to spend some time with children. They will teach you to believe, to love and to play. Children will help you smile from your heart and to have that look of wonderment in your eyes.

"There is a child within everyone. The innocence and the playfulness of a child exists in all human beings. People of all ages like children's stories and while hearing or reading them the child within is invoked. Who does not like to play with children now and then? Watch a ninety year-old man, look at a politician or a government administrator, a business executive or a scientist; all will become playful and free when they are around a child. When he is with his grandchildren or his youngest child, even an old man becomes a child. Crawling on all fours, he pretends he is an elephant. He makes a castle out of playing cards for them. Using sticks and leaves, he builds a play house for the little ones. Bouncing the children on his knee, he tells them that he is a horse.

"Why does he do all this? Is it simply to please the child, to make him or her happy? No. That is not the only reason. It is because in each of us a child is hidden. Somewhere in each one of us, a child's joy, innocence, and faith lie dormant. We delight in searching for the child within. When we were children, we had no worries or problems; recalling these days with love, we want to return to them. This desire is felt by all living beings.

"Children, the wonder and the love that you felt as a child will never return unless you can again play like a child. Innocence is within you, hidden deep inside. You have to rediscover it. And for this to happen, you must go deeper and deeper into your spiritual practices. When you can dive deep into your own consciousness, you will realize this innocence one day. At that moment you will discover the child within you. You will experience the innocence, the joy and the wonder that were hidden inside of you, and you will realize they were always there. You merely forgot your innocence for some time. It is as if you suddenly remember something after having forgotten about it for a very long time. That childlike innocence deep within you is God."

Ammachi, Awaken Children, vol. VI, p. 223

A useful practice for innocence is to look at other people, one by one, and try to imagine how they appeared as seven or eight-year-old children. We can feel that they are still children on the inside, having been draped in older person garments with the passage of time. If they are grumpy or otherwise not innocent in their demeanor, we can still try to see their innocence, realizing that it has gotten lost or buried. We have faith that it is still inside them. Try to see and feel their original innocence. This practice will help us to feel our own innocence and open the gates of our own hearts for love to flow to others.

Instruction from Ammachi

HOW TO PRACTICE DEVOTION

The contents of this chapter are excerpts of *Awaken Children*, by Swami Amritaswarupananda and *Eternal Wisdom* by Swami Jnanamritananda printed with permission of MA Center.

WORSHIPING A FORM

Br: "Amma, is God within or without?"

Mother: "It is only because you have body-consciousness that you think in terms of within and without. In reality, there is no inside or outside. Isn't it because of your sense of 'I' that you think of 'I' and 'you' as being separate? However, as long as the sense of 'I' persists, we can't say that the separation is unreal. God is the vital power that pervades everything. When you visualize Him outside of yourself, you should know that you are, in fact, visualizing what is within you. Nevertheless, it is through such means that the mind is purified."

Br: "There is a special power guiding the universe, but it's hard to believe that it's a God with a certain form."

Mother: "All forms of power are none other than God. He is the all-powerful One who controls everything. If you accept that He is the power behind everything, why can't that power, which controls everything, assume a form that the devotee likes? Why is that difficult to believe?" With great firmness in Her voice Mother continued, "There is a primeval Power in this universe. I look upon the Power as my Mother. That Power is my Mother, and even if I choose to be born again a hundred times, She will continue to be my Mother and I will be Her child. So I cannot make statements such as God has no form."

Ammachi, *Eternal Wisdom*, vol. II, p. 226

Do Deities Exist?

As Mother walked back to the ashram, a brahmachari[1] asked: "Amma, do the deities really exist?"

Mother: "They exist on the subtle plane. Each deity represents a characteristic that is latent within us. But you should view your chosen deity as indistinguishable from the Supreme Self. God can assume any form He wants. God will assume many forms depending on the desires of the devotees. Doesn't the ocean rise up in response to the attraction exerted by the moon?"

Br: "Amma, rather than worshipping the deities whom we have never seen, isn't it best to take refuge in the mahatmas who are alive among us?"

Mother: "Yes. A real tapasvi has the power to assume the burden of our prarabdha.[2] If we take refuge in a mahatma with devotion, our prarabdhas will soon end. One has to make more effort to benefit from worship of the deities, or from temple worship.

"If we worship our chosen deity with the attitude that he is the Supreme Self, we can indeed attain Self-realization. A form is like a ladder. Just as all shadows disappear at high noon, all forms will eventually merge in the formless; but if we take refuge in a satguru, our path will be easier. A guru's help is necessary to remove the obstacles in sadhana, and to show us the way. A guru can help us by clearing our doubts in all crises; then the journey will be easier."

Ammachi, *Eternal Wisdom*, vol. I, p. 192

---

[1] Brahmachari – a celibate practitioner of spiritual disciplines.
[2] Prarabdha – the fruits of actions performed in past lives and also this life which will manifest in this life; karma.

How to Love God

Know that there is nothing in the world but God, that nothing has the power to function without Him. You should see God in everything you touch. When you pick up the clothes that you are going to wear, imagine they are God. And when you pick up your comb, see it as God.

Think of God in the midst of every action you do. And pray, "You are my only refuge. Nothing else is everlasting. No one else's love will last. Worldly love may make me feel good for a while, but ultimately it will only end up hurting me. It's like being caressed by someone with poisonous hands, because in the end such love brings only suffering. No salvation can come from that. Only you, God, can fulfill my yearning." We should pray like this constantly. Without this kind of detachment, we cannot develop spiritually, nor can we help others. We should be firmly convinced that only God is everlasting.

We have to get rid of all the vasanas [mental tendencies] which we have accumulated. But it is difficult to do this all at once. We need constant practice. We should chant our mantra continuously, while sitting, walking, and lying down. By chanting the mantra and visualizing God's form, our other thoughts will fade and our minds will be purified. To wash away the feeling of "I," we need to use the soap of "You." When we perceive that everything is God, the "I" that is, the ego, fades away and the supreme "I" shines forth within us.

Br: "Isn't it difficult to visualize one's Beloved Deity while chanting?"

Mother: "Son, at this moment you are talking to Amma. Does seeing Amma make it difficult to talk to Her? You can talk to Amma and see Her at the same time, can't you? In the same way, we can visualize the form of our Beloved Deity and do japa [repetition of a prayer, a mantra, or one of God's names] at the same time. But even that isn't really needed if you can cry out and pray, 'O Mother, give me strength! Destroy my ignorance! Lift me onto your lap! Your lap is my only refuge; only there will I find peace. Mother, why are you pushing me into this world? I don't want to be without you for a moment. Aren't you the One who gives refuge to everyone? Please be mine! Make my mind your own!' Cry out in this way."

Br: "But I don't feel any devotion. And to be able to pray like that I need to feel devotion, don't I? Amma, you say that we should cry and call out to God, but I first have to feel like crying!"

Mother: "If you can't cry at first, say the words again and again and make yourself cry. A child will pester his mother to make her buy want he wants. He'll keep following her around and he won't stop crying until he has the desired object in his hand. We have to pester the Divine Mother [or your chosen form of God] like that. We have to sit there and cry. Don't give Her a moment of peace! We should cry out, 'Show yourself to me! Show yourself!' Son, when you say that you can't cry, it means that you have no real yearning. Anyone will cry when that longing comes to them. If you can't cry, *make* yourself cry, even if it takes some effort.

"Say that you are hungry but you don't have any food or money. You will go somewhere or do something to get food, won't you? Cry out to the Divine Mother and say, 'Why aren't you giving me tears?' Then She will give you strength, and you will be able to cry. Children, that is what Amma used to do. You can do the same.

"Such tears are not tears of sorrow. They are a form of inner bliss. Those tears will flow when the jivatman (individual soul) merges with the Paramatman (The Supreme Spirit). Our tears mark a moment of oneness with God. Those who are watching us may interpret it as sorrow. For us, however, it is bliss. But you have to do some creative imagination to reach that point. Give it a try, son!"

Br: "I used to meditate on the form of Bhagavan (referring to Krishna). But after meeting Amma that became impossible, because then I couldn't help meditating on Amma's form. Now I can't do that either. Amma, when I think of you, the Lord's form comes to my mind; and when I think of Him, your form appears. I'm unhappy because I can't decide who to meditate on. So now I am not meditating on any form. I meditate on the sound of the mantra."

Mother: "Focus your mind on what appeals to you. Understand that everything is contained in that, and is not separate from you. Whoever or whatever you encounter, know that all are different faces of that one form."

Ammachi, *Eternal Wisdom*, vol. II, p. 38 [brackets by author]

Why Meditate on a Form?

Mother: "Some people say, 'Don't meditate on a form. Brahman has not form, so you should meditate on the Formless.' What sort of logic is that? Normally, we imagine the object of our meditation, don't we? Even if we meditate on a flame or on a sound, it is still based on imagination. What is the difference between that type of meditation and meditation on a form? Those who meditate on the Formless also rely on imagination. Some think of Brahman as pure love, infinitude, or all-pervasiveness. Some repeat, 'I am Brahman,' or inquire, 'Who am I?' But these are still just mental concepts. Thus, it is not truly meditation on Brahman. What, then, is the difference between that and meditating on a form? To bring water to a thirsty man, a container is needed. To realize the formless Brahman, an instrument or a prop is necessary. Also, if we choose to meditate on the Formless, how can we do so without developing love for Brahman? It is therefore nothing but bhakti (devotion). The personal God is nothing but a personification of Brahman."

A brahmachari: "What is the benefit of imagining such a being?"

Mother: "Worship becomes easy when we assign a specific form to Brahman. Then, through our prema (supreme love), we can easily realize the eternal Principle. All the water in a tank can flow out through a single faucet, which allows us to quench our thirst more easily."

Ammachi, *Eternal Wisdom*, vol. II, p. 34

Making the Form Clear

Shastri: "Amma, what should we do to make the form of our Beloved Deity become clear during meditation?"

Mother: "The form becomes clear only when you develop pure love for the deity. As long as you cannot see God, you should be feeling a relentless sense of anguish.

"A sadhak [spiritual aspirant] should have the same attitude towards God as a lover towards his beloved. His love should be such that he cannot bear being separated from God, not even for a moment. If a lover last saw his beloved dressed in blue, then, whenever he sees just a hint of blue anywhere, he sees his beloved and is reminded of her form. While eating and even in his sleep, his mind rests only on her. When he gets up in the morning and brushes his teeth and drinks his coffee, he wonders what she is doing at that moment. This is the kind of love we should have for our Beloved Deity. We shouldn't be able to think about anything else but our object of worship. Even a bitter melon will lose its bitterness and become sweet if it is soaked in sugar for some time. Likewise, a negative mind will be purified if you surrender it to God and think of Him ceaselessly.

"Once, while walking in Vrindavan, a gopi saw a small depression in the ground beneath a tree. She began to imagine, 'Krishna must have come this way! The gopi who was with Him must have asked for a flower from this tree. He held her shoulder for support and then jumped up into the tree. This hole in the ground must be the mark made by His foot as He sprang up.' The gopi called the other gopis and showed them the Lord's footprint. Thinking of the Lord, they completely forgot everything else.

"In the eyes of the gopi, everyone was Krishna. If someone touched her shoulder, she imagined it was Krishna, and in her intense devotion she lost all external consciousness. Whenever the other gopis remembered Krishna, they also became oblivious of their surroundings and shed tears of bliss. We, too, should try to reach that state, associating everything we see with God. For us, there should be no world other than that of God. Then we need to make no special effort to constantly see God in our meditation, because at no time will our minds be without Him.

"Our minds should cry out to everything we see, 'Dear trees and plants, where is my Mother? O birds and animals, have you seen Her? Dear ocean, where is the all-powerful Mother who gives you the power to move?' We can use our imagination in this way. As we persist like this, our minds will break through all obstacles; we will reach the Feet of the Supreme Being and cling to them. Use your imagination in this way. Then the form will definitely become clear in your mind."

Ammachi, *Eternal Wisdom*, vol. II, p. 41 [brackets by author]

GETTING CLEAR FORM TAKES TIME

After the worship was completed, Venu came to sit near the Holy Mother and asked, "Mother, no matter much I try, I am not getting my dhyana rupam (one's form of meditation) clearly. Why is this?"

Mother: "Son, at least a minimum of four years is needed for the form to become full within. In the beginning stages one should try to attain concentration by sitting and looking at the form. If you sit with closed eyes for ten minutes, then the next ten minutes should be spent looking at the picture of one's form of meditation. First external alertness is what is necessary. If there is no alertness in one's external nature it will not be possible to conquer the internal nature (antarika prakriti)."   Ammachi, *Awaken Children*, vol. I, p. 147

HOW TO MEDITATE ON THE FORM

Question: "How should one meditate upon Bhagavan's (the Lord's) form?"

Ammachi: "You should imagine that you are offering flowers at His Feet. When the form fades away, you should imagine that you are mentally embracing the Feet saying, 'Father, why are You going away leaving me alone?' Mentally write 'OM' at His Feet. Otherwise, repeat your mantra and imagine binding the Beloved Deity from toe to head with the rope of japa (repeating the divine name or mantra). Then, imagine that you are undoing this rope. This should be repeated whenever the form fades away. Imagining that the Beloved Deity is standing in front of you, try so see each and every part of the Lord's body. Imagine that you are bathing Him with different things like rose water, coconut water, milk, yogurt, flowers and sacred ash. Adorn His head with a golden crown and put garlands on His neck. Mentally decorate Him with bangles and anklets. Just as the image is decorated in temples, we should adorn our own Beloved Deity. If your Beloved Deity is Devi (the Divine Mother), you should adorn Her with a crown, nose ring, necklaces and other ornaments. She should be dressed in silk clothes. If you do this, the Beloved Deity's form will not escape from your mind. The mind will not get a chance to think about other things. All other thoughts will be restrained. Thus it will become possible to consistently meditate on the Lord's form.

"Children, do not forget to always repeat your mantra. In the beginning japa should be done in a low voice. Later it can be done moving the lips slightly. Finally it should be done mentally. Thus japa should be practiced constantly with each breath. Then japa will go on even if we don't attend to it, even in sleep.

"While walking, imagine that the Beloved Deity is walking by our side and that we are conversing with Him. While riding in a bus, gaze at the sky and imagine that our Beloved Deity is traveling along with us through the sky. If traveling by boat, visualize the Beloved Deity sitting in a fully blossomed lotus on the water. If sitting alone, imagine that the enchanting form of our Beloved Deity is standing at a distance. Through bhavana we should have the feeling that the Lord is always standing near us whatever work we may be doing. While blowing into the oven to kindle the fire, visualize the effulgent form of the Beloved Deity standing in the fire and blow at His Feet. In this way the mind will merge in the Supreme State through constant practice and our efforts will bear fruit."

Ammachi, *Awaken Children*, vol. II, p. 124

Calling You Near

After a fifteen-minute walk they reached the seashore. Mother stood still for quite some time, looking out at the vast expanse of the sea. Then She asked everyone to sit down and meditate. Before they began, Mother gave instructions: "Visualize a fully-bloomed lotus flower in the ocean and imagine that your beloved deity is sitting on it. Try to imagine that the deity is looking at you, smiling at you, calling you near and blessing you. Try to see clearly each and every part of your beloved's form—the eyes, eyebrows, nose, lips, cheeks, forehead, hair, crown, everything. If you don't like to do this, you can simply concentrate on the sound of the ocean waves."

Ammachi, *Awaken Children*, vol. IV, p. 59

The Form Will Become Full of Life

The different stages in meditation are subjectively experienced by the sadhak. Initially one will have to strive hard to focus one's mind on one's Beloved Deity. In the beginning it may not be possible to visualize the full form. Even then, one should not get depressed but should continue one's practice by trying to visualize only the feet of the Deity. In due course, one will be able to visualize the full form. Through the power of persistent practice, the form will become clearer and clearer. As meditation becomes deeper, the form will become full of life and may move and talk to the sadhak. The Beloved Deity may even appear before one whenever requested. This is real "Darshan" or God-vision. One's own spiritual power solidifies by the force of one's resolve and manifests as the Deity. Following this stage is the merging of the sadhak with the Beloved Deity through intense love brought about by constant remembrance of God and the renunciation of every other thought. From there, the Deity Himself will lead one to the final state of Non-dual Experience.

Ammachi, *Awaken Children*, vol. II, p. 261

PLACE A SMALL PICTURE

Student: "Mother, how should we practice meditation?"

Mother: "Place a small picture of a God or Goddess that you like in front of you. Sit gazing at the picture for some time. Then try to fix the form within while closing your eyes. Again look at the external picture when the form within fades away. Again the eyes should be closed. Imagine that you are talking to the Beloved Deity, 'Mother, do not go away abandoning me. Come into my heart. Let me always see Your beautiful form' and so on. Cry, embracing your Beloved Deity. That which we meditate on will appear in front of us if constantly repeated like this with faith."

Ammachi, *Awaken Children*, vol. I, p. 70

IN THE MIDST OF A BLAZING FIRE

There are quite a lot of soot-like stains in our mind. All of that will get washed away when we chant the Divine Name. "You are the All, I am nothing." We should have that kind of love. Otherwise, concentration will not be attained. Son, householders should observe a vow of silence once a week. They should try to get up early in the morning. It is good if they have a regular routine. That will help them to discipline themselves. Until yesterday you were leading a life devoid of spiritual ideals. To get rid of the old habits and replace them with new ones, a regular timetable will be very helpful.

In the beginning you must have love for your daily routine. If you are unable to meditate, try to repeat your mantra. If you find that also to be difficult, then do puja or sing the Divine Names. In whatever way, we must strive hard to attain the constant remembrance of the Supreme. Do not let the mind think unnecessary things. One should meditate by concentrating one's mind on the form of one's Beloved Deity. It is enough to meditate on the feet if it is difficult to meditate on the full form. It is good if meditation is done in dim light. Outside light is a disturbance when we are trying to illuminate our interior.

One should sit gazing at the Beloved Deity's form for two minutes. Then having closed the eyes, visualize the Beloved Deity's form in the heart-lotus. When the form fades away from the heart, one should again gaze at the picture. Though the picture is made of paper and ink, one should imagine that it has consciousness (life). We can attain the Real only through the unreal. Because we are in the unreal, we forget about the Real. We should remember the Real through the man-made picture.

One should cry to God calling thus, "O Mother, where are You? Why did You leave me alone in this forest of materialism? Look, the ferocious animals of lust and anger are coming to eat me. O Mother, take me. Keep me on Your lap. Your lap alone is the safest place for me. Save me from these animals. O Mother, where are You, where are You?"

Our longing to see God should be like the intense desire that we would have to escape if someone were coming to kill us. Our painful longing to see God should be like the pain we would have while dying in the midst of a blazing fire. That much longing should there be to see God. If you are unable to call God the whole day, try at least until noon. You children should find the patience to do this as well.

Ammachi, *Awaken Children*, vol. II, p. 118

LOOK INTO THE WATER

Therefore, children, do not waste these opportunities by talking about silly things. Utilize the time for meditation, silent prayer, and repeating your mantra. Look at the sky and try to visualize the form of your beloved deity there. Try to imagine that He or She is moving with you. Try to see your Ishta Devata's face in the moon or imagine that the moon is the face of the Divine Mother or of Krishna or Rama. As the wind blows try to feel that it is the gentle caress of your beloved deity. Look into the water and visualize the smiling face of your Ishta Devata there. You can imagine that your beloved deity is calling you near, hugging you, kissing you, caressing you, blessing you, and then hiding in the clouds and coming out again a little later. By this kind of imagination you go deeper and deeper into your own consciousness. You enshrine His or Her form within your heart. You open up more and more, and you get closer and closer to your own Self.

Ammachi, *Awaken Children*, vol. VI, p. 110

EVEN REALIZED SOULS SEEK THE SWEETNESS OF BHAKTI

Brahmacharin: "Sri Ramakrishna used to pray, 'O Mother, do not make me mad with Brahmajnana (the knowledge of Brahman). It is enough for me to become Your child.' Why was that?"

Mother: "Form is a ladder on the path of devotion. The devotee loves to be God's servant even after attaining Brahmajnana [knowledge of the absolute]. A true devotee's wish is to continue as such even after attaining the supreme state of Brahmajnana. In order to drink the sweetness of devotion, he will again come down. He will intentionally retain the devotional attitude. No one would be satisfied once they had enjoyed the rasa (essence or sweetness) of bhakti. Didn't Sri Krishna Himself incarnate as Gauranga just to know the rasa of Radha bhava? Children, the sweetness of devotion is something unique.

"Brahman has no name or form. It is infinite like the sky. Knowledge is eternal. When we are in name and form we are in the non-eternal. With his sankalpa [resolve], the devotee can again do rupa dhyana, that is, meditation on the form of his Beloved Deity even after becoming one with the Absolute."

Ammachi, *Awaken Children*, vol. II, p. 148 [brackets by author]

THE NEEDLE AND THE MAGNET
By Sri Ramakrishna

Master: "As the saying goes: 'In my mother's womb I was in a state of yoga [union with God]; coming into the world, I have eaten its clay. The midwife has cut one shackle, the navel cord; but how shall I cut the shackle of maya[3]?

"Maya is nothing but 'woman and gold.'[4] A man attains yoga when he has freed his mind from these two. The Self – the Supreme Self – is the magnet; the individual self is the needle. The individual self experiences the state of yoga when it is attracted by the Supreme Self to Itself. But the magnet cannot attract the needle if the needle is covered with clay; it can draw the needle only when the clay is removed. The clay of 'woman' and 'gold' must be removed."

Mukherji: "How can one remove it?"

Master: "Weep for God with a longing heart. Tears shed for Him will wash away the clay. When you have thus freed yourself from impurity, you will be attracted by the magnet. Only then will you attain yoga."

Mukherji: "Priceless words!"

Master: "If a man is able to weep for God, he will see Him. He will go into samadhi. Perfection in yoga is samadhi. A man achieves kumbhaka[5] without any yogic exercise if he but weeps for God. The next stage is samadhi."

Sri Ramakrishna, *The Gospel of Sri Ramakrishna*, p. 343 [brackets by author]

---

[3] Maya – ignorance preventing the vision of God; the great Cosmic Illusion whereby the many appear out of the One.
[4] Sri Ramakrishna often used the phrase "woman and gold" as a metaphor to include all worldly attachments. To women the phrase would mean "men and gold."
[5] A process in pranayama or breath-control prescribed in hathayoga and rajayoga whereby the breath is retained.

Restlessness for God
By Sri Ramakrishna

Bankim (to the Master): "Sir, how can one develop divine love?"

Master: "Through restlessness – the restlessness a child feels for his mother. The child feels bewildered when he is separated from his mother, and weeps longingly for her. If a man can weep like that for God, he can even see Him."

Sri Ramakrishna, The Gospel of Sri Ramakrishna, p. 674

Persistent Little Boy

As the talk went on, the three-year-old boy started to whimper. He caught hold of his mother's saree and asked for something to eat. Since there weren't any edibles in the car, his mother said, "No, later when we reach home." The child kept quiet for a few moments, then again caught hold of her saree and repeated the same request. Now the mother became a bit angry and said, "Keep quiet. Let me listen to Mother's words." But the child was hungry and couldn't keep quiet. After a few seconds he began crying out, "I want something to eat. I want something, I want something to eat." The mother this time became really angry and hit the child, pulling his hand from her saree. Now the child fell on his mother's lap bursting into tears, calling "Amma…Amma…." Now the mother's face bloomed with love and affection for her child. Embracing him tightly and kissing both his cheeks several times, she consoled him uttering soothing words like, "Mother's darling son…little thief, don't cry…" She asked the driver to stop the car and get some bananas for him. This was done immediately.

Now the Holy Mother turned toward Balu and said, "Did you see that? This is the correct attitude that a true seeker or devotee should have toward God or Guru. He may scold you or kick you out but don't loosen the hold. Like this innocent child, go on calling Him with more and more intensity. Go on asking while catching hold of His feet. The relationship of the child to his mother is so strong that he didn't feel any hatred or anger toward her. Instead, he tightened his hold and finally laid down on her lap when she hit him. This was enough for the hidden compassion of the mother to overflow all its bounds. Son, this is the kind of attachment that a sadhak should have toward God. Whatever happens, hold on to His feet without loosening the grip even slightly. Then He is bound to shower His grace. Love with attachment to God is good but not with attachment to the world."

Ammachi and Swami Amritaswarupananda, *Awaken Children*, vol. I, p. 106

CRY FOR GOD

"Amma feels sad because Her children aren't trying hard enough to make their minds one-pointed. Cry out for God. Only by crying for Him will your minds become one-pointed. Nothing is possible without devotion for God. A true devotee doesn't even yearn for liberation. Devotion is even higher than liberation. A devotee always experiences the bliss of his love for God. What, then, is the need for liberation?   The devotee is in constant bliss while in this world, so why would he want to think about any other world?"

Mother showed the tip of one of Her fingers. "In front of bhakti, mukti (liberation) is no more than this."

Mother took a sip from a cup of coffee which had been placed in front of Her by a brahmachari. Getting up with the cup in Her hand, She poured a little coffee into everyone's mouth. As She poured the coffee, She whispered in each person's ear, "My child, call out to God and cry! Cry for God, my child!"

Ammachi, *Eternal Wisdom*, vol. II, p. 194

SAVED BY A FEW TEARS

Mother: "Children, the tears that flow when one prays to God with love are not tears of sorrow; they are tears of bliss. Nowadays, people pray to God only during times of distress. If you pray to God in times of both happiness and sadness, you will no longer have to experience any suffering. Even if some suffering should come to you, it won't appear as suffering. God will look after you. If you can pray to Him with an open heart and shed a few tears out of love for Him, then you are saved."

Ammachi, *Eternal Wisdom*, vol. II, p. 72

CRY AND PRAY TO GOD

Amma was giving darshan in the hut. One of the devotees asked, "Amma, I know only a little about spirituality. I have faith in Mother and I want to lead a devoted and dedicated life. Could you please tell me something about becoming more spiritual?"

Mother gave him this answer: "Son, first of all, you should give up this idea about becoming more spiritual. Just try to pray sincerely to God and meditate on Him. Don't think about becoming more spiritual. That very thought can sometimes be a hindrance.

"Cry and pray to God. Sing His glories. Don't overstrain yourself to try to sit in lotus posture or hold your breath to mediate on His form. Meditation is remembrance of God, constant and loving remembrance. Consider Him as your beloved or just consider yourself as His child. Or consider Him as your father or mother. Simply try to think of Him just as we think of our father or mother or beloved. How does a lover remember his beloved? Certainly not by sitting in lotus posture. The remembrance simply happens in him while he is lying down, walking or sitting on the banks of a river, or it may happen while he is at work. It does not matter where he is or what he is doing. Likewise, remember your beloved deity whenever you can, no matter where you are or what you are doing.

"Contemplate Him as your creator, protector and the final abode to where you will return. Try to feel Him with your heart; try to feel His presence, grace, compassion and love. Open your heart and pray to Him, 'O Lord, my creator, protector, and final resting place, guide me to Your light and love. Fill my heart with Your presence. I've been told that I am Your child, but I am totally ignorant of my existence in You. My most beloved Lord, I do not know how to worship You, or how to please You or meditate on Your form. I have not studied the scriptures: I know not how to glorify You. O Compassionate One, show me the right path so that I can return to my real abode which is nothing but You.'

"Children, pray and shed tears as you think of Him. That is the greatest sadhana (spiritual practice). No other sadhana will give you the bliss of divine love as effectively as sincere prayer. You don't have to undergo any academic training to love God. You don't have to be a scholar or a philosopher to worship Him or to call out to Him. Just call out, but let the call come from your heart. Just as a child cries out for food or to be fondled or cuddled by his mother, call out to Him with the same intensity and innocence. Cry and pray to Him. He must reveal Himself. He cannot sit silent and unmoved when somebody calls Him like that.

"Children, innocent prayer, calling out to the Lord, is a very power-ful way to please the Lord. You don't need to be a scholar to do that. Even for an unschooled layman or an illiterate forest dweller, the Lord's grace can be attained if one is really determined to achieve the goal." Ammachi, *Awaken Children*, vol. 5, p. 19

VALUE OF CRYING TO GOD

One of the brahmacharins who was present during the afternoon conversation asked, "Amma, this afternoon you instructed a young man just to pray and cry for God. Is that enough to know God?"

"Yes," Mother said, "if performed with all one's heart. Son, don't think that spiritual practice is only sitting in lotus posture and medi-tating or repeating a mantra. Of course, those too are ways, tech-niques to remember God and to know the Self. They certainly will help to train and tame the naturally restless body and mind. But it is wrong to think these practices alone are the way.

"Take, for example, the Gopis of Brindavan and Mirabai. What was their sadhana? How did they become Krishnamayis (full of Krishna)? Was it through long hours of sitting in lotus posture doing rigorous meditation? No. But of course they did meditate. They did constant and intense meditation, but not sitting with crossed legs. Devotees like the Gopis and Mirabai constantly remembered the glories of the Lord, cherishing His Divine Form within themselves, irrespective of time or place. They just cried and cried until their tears washed away their entire mind-stuff, until all their thoughts were gone.

"Children, when we cry we can forget everything effortlessly. Crying helps us to stop brooding on the past and dreaming about the future. It helps us to be in the present—with the Lord and His Divine leela.

Suppose someone very dear to us dies—say our mother or father, wife or husband, or a son or daughter. We will lament, thinking of him or her, won't we? We forget everything else. At that moment nothing else comes to our minds except the sweet memories of the departed one. We will have no other interest than thinking about and contemplating that person. Our minds become fully focused on that person.

"Children, crying has the power to make the mind completely one-pointed. Why do we meditate? To get concentration, isn't that why? Yes. So, the best way to get concentration is by crying to the Lord. That is a very powerful way of remembering God, and that in fact is meditation. That is what great devotees like the Gopis and Mirabai did. See how selflessly Mirabai prayed, 'O Mira's Giridhari, it does not matter if You don't love me. But, O Lord, please do not take away my right to love You.' They prayed and cried until their whole being was transformed into a state of constant prayer. They kept on worshipping the Lord until they were totally consumed by the flames of Divine Love. They themselves became the offering.

"Once you become the offering, once your whole being is in a state of constant prayer, then what is left is not you but Him. What is left is Love. Prayer can perform this miracle. Crying can accomplish this feat. What is the purpose of meditation? It is to become love. It is to attain Oneness. Thus there is no better meditation technique than praying and crying to the Lord.

"Supplicate Him. Pour out your heart to Him. Prayer is nothing but emptying the mind, ridding oneself of the vasanas. Prayer is nothing but accepting His supremacy and remembering your own nothing-ness. 'I am nothing. I am nobody. You are everything.' Prayer teaches us humility. You are seeking His refuge, His love, His grace, compassion and help, in order to reach Him. You are calling out, trying to reach out. Prayer is surrendering the ego. From deep within you are trying to reach out. You are trying to become expansive. You tell the Lord, 'O Lord, I have no power. I thought I had, but now I understand that I am helpless. I am in the dark. I cannot see. I am nothing...Guide me, lead me, help me. That was my ego which made me think I was something great. Now I realize that I am helpless. Without Your grace I cannot be anything....' What is this? This is exposing yourself as a totally helpless creature without

Him and His Grace. This is humbling yourself. This is the genuine way to exhaust the vasanas. There should be the awareness of helplessness; one should feel one's helplessness. Helplessness will make one humble. Humility in turn will help one get God's grace as well as human love." Ammachi, *Awaken Children*, vol. 5, p. 29

Abandon the World - Cry to God

"There is no point in strutting about making a display of one's devotion to the Guru and prayers to God. Sincerity is needed. One should cry and pray to God thus: 'O Lord, don't You see me lying down below? O Lord, shower Your grace upon me through Your Hands of thousands and thousands of stars. O Lord, please give me the strength to remember You always. O Lord, give me sorrow so that I will constantly remember You. You alone are my refuge and consolation. How blissful is Your divine world! How beautiful it is! Lift me to Your world of thousands of twinkling stars. Do You not see the ferocious animals of lust and greed coming to swallow me? Are You not seeing me enveloped by poisonous germs and enduring tortures?' Such prayers will quickly bear fruit."

Ammachi, *Awaken Children*, vol. II, p. 341

Real Love Should Be There

Recollecting the days she had spent in a God-intoxicated mood, the Holy Mother revealed, "This open ground served Mother a lot during those days. Ah, the time which I spent dancing and singing in bliss is incomparable..." Suddenly, she went into samadhi. Tears of bliss rolled down her cheeks. With her eyes fixed somewhere in a boundless dimension, she sat as still as a statue for quite some time. Slowly coming down, Mother again related, "It is always very difficult to remember those days. It will steal away all my external consciousness. The sweetness and bliss bestowed by desireless devotion is something unique. Though advaita (the state of non-duality) is the Ultimate Truth, Mother sometimes feels that it is all meaningless and would like to remain like a child in front of God. There are people who preach the advaita philosophy, but this will not help much to progress spiritually, even though it does give a certain amount of intellectual understanding. For people to have a glimpse and a taste of spiritual life, devotion and love for the Supreme is absolutely necessary. Not mere devotion, but real love should be there."

One devotee: "Mother, how can one make that differentiation? What do you mean by 'mere devotion' and what is 'real love?'"

Amma: "Son, devotion can sometimes be like a mere performance of one's duty. For example, in this village, in almost all the houses you can see people chanting and singing every day at dusk, reading the Bhagavata and the Ramayana and other holy books when they get the time, and so forth. But are they doing it with intense love and longing to see the Lord? There are many people who simply do it as a duty."   Ammachi, *Awaken Children*, vol. III, p. 60

REAL BHAKTI

Amma: "Mere bhakti is not sufficient. Love is needed. Only then will the mind get absorption."

Question: "In the light of what you said just now, it sounds to me that devotion (bhakti) and love (prema) are two different things."

Amma: "Son, look, this is how it can be differentiated. Devotion is praying and supplicating to God just to satisfy one's selfish motives and desires. Such people will generally cling to temples. Even if they do go to see Mahatmas, they will be very keen to present before the Mahatma all the problems that they have. Such people have devotion, but pure love is at a minimum in their devotion. They give suggestions or instructions to God or to the Mahatma, such as 'My Lord, this is my desire. Please fulfill it,' or 'I don't want that to occur. Don't make it happen.' They want Him to act according to their own wishes and their own wills. They think they know more than He does. Their understanding about God or the Mahatma is far inferior to that of a devotee endowed with pure love, who loves God or the Guru for love's own sake. Such a person endowed with love wants nothing, not even Liberation. He simply wants to love God or the Guru, no matter what happens. To love Him is his happiness. He wants to cast off all his desires except the desire to love Him.

"Therefore, bhakti (devotion) endowed with prema (love) is prema bhakti. Bhakti bereft of prema is mere devotion. Both a person with prema bhakti and a person with only bhakti will love the Guru or God, but the one with prema bhakti will give all importance to God or Guru; he has no choices, no wish or will of his own. His Guru is everything for him. He simply wants to love him, surrender to him, forgetting everything else. He wants to be consumed by the flame of the love which he has towards his Guru or Beloved Deity.

"However, for the second type of bhakti, what is of primary importance is himself. He first wants to fulfill all his desires, then he thinks of God. As far as he is concerned, God or the Guru is like an agent to fulfill his desires."

Ammachi, Awaken Children, vol. III, p.106

LIKE LOVE BETWEEN A MAN AND A WOMAN

If we have true devotion, we can see the form of our Beloved Deity in the statue installed in the inner sanctum of the temple. Suppose we sincerely love a lady. Whichever woman we see or meet, we will be reminded of our Beloved. Sometimes there will be a slight resemblance. At other times there will not be any at all. Even then, we will think and imagine that this girl's nose is like hers, and that girl walks like her, and this girl's eyes are exactly like hers, and that girl's hair is like hers; we will imagine in this way. Likewise, when we see somebody else's child, we will attribute similarities such as, this child smiles like my child. Even if there are no similarities, out of love we will feel as if there were. In a similar manner, one who has sincere love for God will see His form everywhere. If it is not there, he will imagine his Beloved everywhere. That is how real love should be.

Suppose a young man goes to the office. He has a deep love for a woman. He thinks, "She may be taking a bath now. Now she may be having her breakfast, and now she may be going to the college," and so on. Thus his mind will be completely on her. Then he will think, "She will be holding her books like this." Thinking and imagining in this fashion, he holds the briefcase in his hand in the same way as he imagines the girl would hold her textbooks; so much does she saturate his thoughts. Even while sitting in the bus, he may think about her. He will not be aware of the other things happening in the bus, whatever they may be. All of his mind is on the lady whom he loves. For us, this kind of love should go towards God. Because of his thoughts about her, even his ways will become like hers. Eventually he himself will become her, just as Radha became Krishna by always thinking of Him.

Ammachi, Awaken Children, vol. II, p. 31

CONSTANT REMEMBRANCE

Amma: "Children, you should develop an attitude of bowing down to anything and everything. Keep the plate of food in front of you and bow down to the food before eating and bow down to the plate after eating. An attitude to prostrate to anything at any time should come. In this way, an awareness, 'for what am I doing this,' will arise. Thus we should build up good character. Prostrate to the cloth you will wear. Bow down to the water with which you will take a shower. During these occasions of bowing down, you will have a pure resolve to see the same consciousness in everything whether with form or without. While doing so, you are in fact re-membering God. While taking a shower, imagine that you are doing so with the Lord. Even if you are on the toilet, imagine that you are talking to Him. Do not waste any time. Simply do it. Constant re-membrance of God, irrespective of time and place, is real devotion. If you practice in this manner, He will come; He must come. God will come and play with you. Imagine that you are talking to Him while performing any action, whatever it is.

"Thus, as your imagination and resolve become stronger and stron-ger, you can slowly feel His presence, both inside and outside. The vague presence in the beginning will culminate into a constant expe-rience in due course, because of your incessant practice.

"Constant remembrance of God, irrespective of time and place, is real devotion. If you practice in this manner, He will come; He must come. God will come and play with you."

Ammachi, Awaken Children, vol. III, p. 320

Leaky Hose

As the Holy Mother was sitting conversing with the devotees, one brahmacharin came holding a hose to water the plants. However, the water pressure was very little. Mother looked at it and noticed that there were many holes in the hose through which the water was leaking out. Pointing to the hose She said, "Look at that, children. Because there are holes in the hose, the water is not coming out properly. Likewise, progress will not be gained in meditation if the mind is dissipated through worldly thoughts. At present, whatever spiritual power is gained through meditation and other spiritual practices gets dissipated through indulgence. It is like drawing water from a well in a bucket full of holes. All the water will leak out by the time the bucket reaches the top of the well. As we do spiritual practice, we should take care to control the urge for worldly pleasures. That Supreme Effulgence can be known through intuitive experience only if the mind is made one-pointed without sending it out to the world. Meditation can be done while fixing the mind either between the eyebrows or in the heart. If someone has no faith in God or in a form of God, they can make their mind one-pointed by fixing it on a point or on any part of their own body. One should continue doing meditation with the conviction that one's Beloved Deity is in one's own heart. One may get a headache and pain in the eyes if one meditates on the spot between the eyebrows. Insomnia also may occur. If so, meditation should be stopped temporarily. If restlessness occurs, then it is best to meditate in the heart. In the beginning it is better to meditate in the heart. After having the feeling that the heart is full, it is not so dangerous if meditation is shifted to the spot between the eyebrows. In any case, it is best for householders to meditate in the heart. One will feel a cooling effect by meditating in the heart, whereas heat is experienced if one meditates between the eyebrows." Ammachi, *Awaken Children*, vol. II, p. 123

Why Bhakti is Best for Western Children

"Many problems will arise if only one path is prescribed for all. Real spiritual growth will not take place if a person who is supposed to follow the path of devotion is told to take the path of Raja Yoga. It is like telling an asthma patient to take medicine for diabetes. Being advised to take a path not appropriate for them is a stumbling block for many people in their spiritual quest. Mother cannot say that one path alone is good enough for everyone in order to attain the goal.

"But generally speaking, the Path of Devotion is the easiest and the least complicated. While anybody can love, not all can do pranayama (breath control) or Hatha Yoga (yogic postures). Only certain people endowed with a certain mental and physical constitution can do these. But love has no prerequisites. Whoever has a heart can love, and everyone has a heart. To love is an innate tendency in human beings. However, we cannot say that pranayama or Hatha Yoga come naturally to human beings. Bhakti is love – loving God, loving your own Self, and loving all beings. The small heart should become bigger and bigger and, eventually, totally expansive. A spark can become a forest fire. So to have only a spark is enough, for the spark is also fire. Keep blowing on it, fanning it. Sooner or later it will burn like a forest fire, sending out long tongues of flame. At present, love is like a spark within us. Constantly blow on it, using the fan of the Divine Name, japa and meditation. You may perspire, sneeze and cough, but do not stop. Your body may become hot; tears may fill your eyes; you may want to faint. But do not stop. If you perspire, you sneeze and cough, persist in your efforts, and be assured then that you are heading towards the goal. Soon you will become Love itself. This is the reward for your love.

"The Path of Love, otherwise known as the Path of Devotion, is the best one for Western children. Of course, this is a general statement. In the West, society is such that people, even from early childhood, are intellectual and take an intellectual approach to everything. It is the product of their 'modern' education. They are fed with all kinds of factual information about the empirical world, and the emphasis is on science and technology. So their analytical minds are well-developed, but their hearts are dry. In most cases, the hearts of people in the West remain under-developed and imperfect. The head is big, but the heart is shriveled up and dry."

"What is the cause for this dryness?" the Western man further asked.

Mother elaborated, "The social norm that prevails paves the way for this dryness of the heart. One gets one's first lessons in love from one's mother. But in the West, the roles of mother and father become confused. Mothers become fathers and thus lose the quality of motherly love. They have no real love for their children. The instability of married life is another factor. The husband-wife and the mother-father relationship is so weak and fragile. A child who lives in this kind of situation cannot be loving. He or she cannot be affectionate. Such children do not even learn the most basic lessons of love. Of course, love cannot be taught like one can be taught to read and write. What Mother means is that there are no proper circumstances created for them to develop love in their lives. They grow up seeing the conflicts, arguments, disputes, hatred, fighting and finally the separation of their parents. They never experience what love is, which is what they are supposed to learn from the mutual love between their father and mother. The parents are the two Gurus which the children see from birth until they come into contact with the world. If the seed of love is not sown at home, it cannot sprout or blossom.

"The Path of Bhakti teaches love. First, you develop one-pointed love toward God. When that love becomes the center of your life and as the devotional practices become more and more intense, your vision changes. You come to understand that God dwells as Pure Consciousness in all beings, including you. As this experience becomes stronger and stronger, the love in you also grows until at last you become That. The love within you expands and embraces the entire universe with all its beings. You become the personification of Love. This Love removes all dryness from you. This Love is the best cure for all emotional blocks and for all negative feelings. Therefore, Mother thinks that the Path of Love is the best for Western seekers." Ammachi, *Awaken Children*, vol. IV, p. 142

MANY ADVANTAGES TO THE PRACTICE OF BHAKTI

"Amma, why does Amma place so much importance on the path of devotion?"

"Children," She began, "there are many reasons why we should consider the path of devotion the most suitable path for most people. First of all, it gives much contentment to the practitioner. A contented person will have enthusiasm and vigor. He will be very optimistic and endowed with an adventurous mind. His attitude is that life and everything that happens in life is a gift, and this gives him immense patience and strength. Unlike those who pursue other paths, he does not believe that happiness is a right to which he is entitled. As far as he is concerned, there are no rights, there are only gifts. This attitude helps him to accept everything as a gift, both good and bad, and also instills him with courage and faith. Such a person will have a loving and compassionate heart, a child-like innocence, and a pleasing nature. Not wanting to injure anyone or hurt anybody's feelings, he cannot harm anyone. He will also have the power to renounce his comforts and pleasures for the happiness and peace of others. He will experience the same problems in life as everyone else, but he will have the mental ability and balance to remain calm and quiet when adversity arises. He practices acceptance, for his attitude is that life and everything that happens in life is a gift, not a right.

"Such a person derives his power to be content and relaxed from his unshakable faith in and love toward the Supreme Power. And he will have a name and form for this Supreme Power. He may call it Krishna, or he may call it Christ or Buddha. The power of the name that he chants, and the mental image of the form he cherishes, as well as his faith that his Lord is always with him and protects him from all dangers, helps him to be content, relaxed, optimistic and cheerful at all times and in all circumstances.

"Take, for example, the Gopas and Gopis of Brindavan. They were always blissful and happy, full of vigor and cheer. All the work they did carried a special charm and beauty of its own. They were always in a festive mood, and one could see only happy and contented faces all around, for their lives were sparkling with joy. Life was a festival for them, and idleness was non-existent as they sang and danced with great joy while performing any work. Even their customary chores of taking the cows to the meadows, milking them, and selling the milk and butter became blissful work. They had extraordinary strength and courage, and if they had problems, they confronted them most courageously. Always adventurous and loving in nature, they lived life to its fullest.

"What was the source of their contentment and joy? Their faith in their Beloved Lord Krishna. It was their faith in His omnipotence and their adoration of Him that helped them celebrate all of life. They became fearless and courageous in His presence. So, children, devotion and love for God is the way to contentment. That alone is the way to peace, happiness, courage and fearlessness. Such qualities that help bring us the fullness of life are not easily available to people who practice other paths.

"Look at Hanuman, the great devotee of Lord Sri Rama. He stands as a magnificent example of tireless work, inexhaustible energy and a being of great achievements. There was not a single incident when Hanuman said 'no' to anything he was asked to do. Obstacles were nothing to him. Whenever Rama was struck with a tragic incident, Hanuman was by His side to carry out His commands. Even the seemingly impossible became possible through Hanuman's constant effort, determination and unshakable faith. He was the embodiment of strength, courage, vigor, fearlessness, determination, optimism, discrimination and contentment. Yet he remained Sri Rama's simple and humble devotee, completely surrendered at the Feet of his Lord.

"Contentment ensues from egolessness. And egolessness comes from devotion, love, and utter surrender to the Supreme Lord. Egoistic people cannot be content or happy. They are tense because they have fear, and this fear makes them almost crazy. Most of the time such people are hungry for power, and that craving makes them blind. They want to grab and possess everything, not caring if they use mean and wicked ways, not caring if they ruin other people. The constant fear that they will be deprived of their power and possessions haunts them, and increases their fear and discontent. Look at all the dictators of the world. They are the most egotistic people. Craving power and position, they are war-mongers with no concern for the peace and happiness of society. They don't even care about their own wives and children. They are concerned only about themselves and what will happen to them tomorrow and in the future. They have no qualms about what evil means they may use to gain power. Tense with their own discontentment, they carry negativity around with them and spread it to others. Thus everyone, every single soul around them is made unhappy and discontent.

"Hiranyakasipu, Prahlada's father, was a typical example of someone who abused power. Children, by looking at his life, you will get a very good picture of how an extremely egotistic person is totally lacking in compassion. Such a person is full of discontent, anger, fear and cruelty. Hiranyakasipu even tried to kill Prahlada, his son, just to protect his own power, name and fame. But look at Prahlada. In all adversities, he was calm and unmoved like a mountain. He was fearless, courageous, and always content. Why? Because he was a true devotee of God. His joy didn't leave him even when he was thrown into the ocean or was condemned to death by being trampled by a mad elephant or burned alive. Through all of this he remained calm and unperturbed. He was content with whatever happened, good or bad, because he considered life and everything that happened in life as a gift from God. All true devotees have this attitude.

"Contentment comes only when you are surrendered, only when you have the attitude of complete acceptance. It arises only when you can welcome impartially every experience in life. You can be fully content when you can smile at and even welcome death. And even if surrender does not happen immediately, one must at least have the willingness to surrender to the Supreme Will. Only then will one be able to enter into that state of everlasting contentment. If one develops this attitude of acceptance, the moment will eventually come when one becomes eternally content. Do not idle away your time in waiting for contentment. Nothing will happen. Discontent will prevail in a person who waits without doing anything. Prepare your mind and try to develop the willingness to accept and surrender. Try to welcome and receive both the good and bad. Try to build up an attitude that allows you to smile even at death. This is the way to contentment."   Ammachi, *Awaken Children*, vol. VI, p. 126

Attitude of Renunciation (Detachment)

Another brahmacharin asked, "Amma, while talking about contentment, You said that real contentment can arise only when one understands the spiritual aspect of devotion, and only when one has renunciation. What do you mean by that?"

Amma replied, "The word renunciation scares some people. Their attitude is that if contentment can come only through giving up, then it is better not to be content. They wonder how they can lead a contented life without wealth, without a beautiful house, a nice car, a wife or husband, without all the conveniences and comforts of life? Without all these, life would be impossible, it would be hell, they think.

"But do you know anyone whose possessions make them really happy and content? People who look for happiness in life's many conveniences and comforts are the most miserable ones. The more wealth and comforts one has, the more worries and problems one will have. The more one desires, the more one will feel discontent, because desires are endless. The chain of greed and selfishness continues to lengthen. It is an endless chain. A person who is always thinking about accumulating more and more and more cannot be content. This does not mean that in order to be content one should never want to fulfill any desire. That is not the point. The point is that one should learn to be content with what one has. To merely acquire more wealth and to seek honor and status should not be life's sole aim. Plow the field, sow the seeds, take good care of the seedlings, remove the weeds, give water and manure, and then wait patiently. If all this is done well and with an attitude of self-surrender and love, there will be a bountiful harvest. All actions bear fruit. The future is the fruit. But don't worry about the future. Wait patiently, dwelling in the present, performing your actions with concentration and love. Action is the present. Love each action; find bliss in all that you do. That is the most important thing. When you can live in each moment of action, good results must come.

"Only by living in the present can one fully enjoy what one has. This means that you must stop getting anxious about the results of your actions, and stop worrying about things that have been done in the past. Real renunciation is the renunciation of the past and the future. The past is the garbage can where you have dumped all the actions you have performed. It is a storehouse of everything good and bad. The past is a wound. Don't touch it or scratch it. Don't make it bigger. If you scratch the wound–that is, if you delve into your memories–the wound will get infected. Don't do that. Try instead to let it heal. Healing is possible only through faith and love of God. This is possible only in the present. Remember God, chant His name, meditate on His form, and repeat your mantra. That is the best medicine to heal the wound of the past. Take that medicine to forget the past and do not be anxious about the future.

"Real devotion requires renunciation. This is what most so-called devotees lack. Such a devotee constantly broods over the past, or he dreams about the future, building castles in the air. Even while chanting God's name, he is lost in past memories or creating some future dream. Thus, he misses the beauty of chanting God's name. He does not appreciate the divine beauty of his beloved deity or his Guru's compassionate and loving form, and thus misses the Grace as well. His prayers are empty; he never looks into his own heart. He never enjoys the ecstasy of devotion and love. Lacking absorption, his meditations are dry. Because he can renounce neither the past nor the future, he misses the beauty of the present. His actions are not beautiful. His words cannot inspire.

"Living in the present is the spiritual aspect of devotion. The so-called devotee is more concerned about the material aspect of his faith. For him faith in God is a part-time business. His prayers and meditations are not real. He cannot let go. He is so attached that he sometimes even calls out, 'Oh, I cannot forget my memories! They are grabbing me, binding me.' What a pity! Memories cannot bind him. They are inert and lifeless. They have no power of their own. It is he who gives power to them; it is he who grabs at them. If he would just release his grip, he would be free. He philosophizes a lot about renunciation and selflessness, but he is not sincere."

Ammachi, *Awaken Children*, vol. VI, p. 150

ATTITUDE OF SURRENDER

Student: "Mother, there are many people who still experience sorrow even after crying to God."

Mother: "We call God with many desires. The mind is filled with desires, not with God's Form. That means that we see God as a laborer. It should not be like that. Even if God is the servant of His devotees, it is not correct for us to see Him as such. Dedicate everything at His Feet. We must have the attitude of surrender, then He will definitely protect us. Even after getting into the boat or bus, you won't carry the luggage, will you? You will put it down. Likewise, surrender everything to God. He will protect us. Have the thought that God is near us. If there is a place to rest nearby, the mere thought of unloading the luggage which we are carrying on our head lessens the weight of the burden. If we think that there is no place to rest, then the baggage seems heavier. In the same way, when we think that God is near, all our burdens diminish."

Ammachi, Awaken Children, vol. I, p. 6

DEVOTIONAL SINGING IN THIS AGE

A group of devoted women were sitting around the Holy Mother. A few of them had taken a course on Vedanta. Mother said to them, "The goal is Jnana and the means is bhakti. Children, bhakti is the path to Jnana. Devotion with love for God should arise. In this age, more concentration is gained through kirtan [devotional singing] than through dhyana (meditation). The present atmosphere is always filled with different kinds of sound. Because of that, dhyana will be difficult. Concentration will not be gained easily. This can be overcome if kirtan is performed. Not only that, the atmosphere will also become pure. Innocence will arise if one travels on the bhakti marga (path of devotion). All can be seen with the attitude of brotherhood."   Ammachi, *Awaken Children*, vol. I, p. 142

SING WITH LOVE AND DEVOTION

The Mother abruptly stopped singing, feeling that some of the brahmacharins were singing without love and devotion.

Amma: (In a serious tone) "Other than losing the power that you acquire through meditation, bhajan serves no purpose if it is not sung with concentration and love. Do not sing if you cannot sing with concentration. If the bhajan is sung with one-pointedness, it is beneficial for the singer, the listeners, and Nature as well. Later when the listeners reflect on the songs, they will try to live in accordance with the lessons enunciated therein. Bhajans should be sung with eyes closed. You should hear the song you yourself are singing and grasp its meaning. While singing, you should imagine that your Beloved Deity is listening to the song while sitting in your heart or standing before you. You should be able to shed at least one tear at the Lord's Feet while singing. During Mother's sadhana, She could not even utter the names of Krishna or Devi. If She did so, She would immediately become lost to this world. Mother desires to see Her children crying for God. That is how you can make Mother happy."

Having said these words, the Mother sang the rest of the song. The atmosphere became saturated with spiritual vibrations. It seemed that the Mother's instructions went straight into everyone's heart. They all lost themselves in the glory of chanting the Divine Name.

Ammachi, *Awaken Children*, vol. II, p. 324

Chanting the Divine Name

Question: "Mother, can one attain God by merely chanting the Divine Name?"

Amma: "Certainly, why doubt? But concentration is a must. Kirtan (singing the Divine Name) is the best way for householders. Having closed the door, one should imagine that one's beloved Deity is standing everywhere in the room. Then one should pray thus, 'O Lord, are You not seeing me? O God, please take me on Your lap. I am Your child. I have no one but You as my refuge. Do not abandon me but always dwell in my heart.' Surrender all that we have to Bhagavan (the Lord). We will go to the railway station when we travel, carrying heavy loads. After getting into the train, we do not continue to carry the luggage on our head. Having unloaded it, we comfortably sit in our seat, don't we? Once faith in God arises, then surrender everything at His Feet. We should live with the attitude that He will protect us. Everything is His, nothing is mine, He will take care of everything. We have to think this way. A real parent is one who can create children and save them from death. Are we able to create children? If we can, then we should be able to bring back to life those children who die. But, of course, we cannot. Only God is the Giver of life and Creator of the world and all its beings. Therefore, the real father and mother is God. Others are only foster parents.

"We have no control over the things or objects that we claim as ours. We have no control even over our own body or existence. Then what can we say about other things? How can we say that a thing which is not under our control is ours? Neither the creation of an object nor its sustenance or destruction is in our hands. Yet, foolishly we think that it is ours. Therefore, dedicate everything to God. We should always feel, 'O Lord, I am just a puppet in Your hands. You are the one who gives me power. Even a blade of grass will not move without Your Power.' We should pray with longing, 'O Lord, where are You, where are You? Wash away my ignorance. Wash away my ego.'" Ammachi, *Awaken Children*, vol. II, p. 115

AMMA'S DIVINE MOODS

SHE STRUGGLES TO STAY DOWN

The Mother sometimes would cry, and at other times, She would burst into ecstatic laughter. At a certain point She drew within and became totally absorbed while the brahmacharins took over the lead singing. Next Her gestures were like those of an innocent child in supplication to its mother. With both hands raised, She called out, "Amma...Amma.... Where are You?" or "Hey, Kali.... Kali! Come here."

With this kind of supreme devotion, different aspects and different layers of the Supreme Consciousness appeared, disappeared and reappeared in the manifestations of the Mother's body. Perched on those wings of divinity, everyone present passed beyond the ordinary to the blissful world of supreme love and devotion. As She sang, one could see the Mother wiping tears every now and then.

Whenever She talks about the path of devotion, Amma says, "Look, children, Mother knows very well that all names and forms are limited and that God is nameless, formless and attributeless. Still, the sweet and blissful feeling that one has from singing the glories of the Lord is an incomparable and inexpressible experience. While singing to the Lord, it is very difficult for Mother to control the mind and bring it down. On such occasions She may become mad with Divine Love. It is a real struggle to keep the mind down. Therefore, Mother puts on a temporary veil which can be removed at any time. It is this veil which helps the mind to remain in this physical plane. This veil can be removed by mere will whenever Mother wants.

Children, innocent love can easily take us to that inexpressible experience. Therefore, try to develop that love in your heart."
Ammachi, Swami Amritaswarupananda, *Awaken Children*, vol. IV, p. 257

THE BLISS-INTOXICATED DIVINE MOOD

At six-thirty in the evening the residents began the singing of
bhajans. After a few songs, Brahmacharin Balu started singing
Saranagati (O Mother, Give Refuge). By the time the Holy Mother
came to join in, the same song was still being sung since it was a
long bhajan. She took over the lead singing.

> O Light that illumines the whole Universe
> And even the sun, moon and the stars;
> O Primordial Nature,
> Governess of the entire Universe,
> O Universal Mother, who is the Incarnation
> Of pure and selfless Love,
> This destitute cries for Thy vision
> With a heart endowed with intense yearning.

The Mother was unusually enraptured with the bliss of Divine Love.
She swayed vigorously from side to side, back and forth. An inexpressible and indescribably beautiful blending of the diverse aspects
of supreme devotion and love slowly manifested in the Mother. It
enveloped each and every person present. Through the Divine voice
of the Holy Mother the song attained wings. It soared up and
flowed like a never-ending stream as the song continued,

> O Mother, the ocean sings Thy Glory
> Through the resounding of the Sacred Syllable,
> Aum...one after the other,
> Each and every wave dances gleefully
> In time with the Pranava, the Primordial Sound,
> Aum...

With a voice full of feeling and a heart full of longing, the Mother
called out, "Amme...Amme..." Her eyes were fixed on the sky
above and her hands were outstretched. The Mother's call was so
full of love and authenticity that it gave the feeling to everyone that

the Divine Mother Herself was standing in front of the Holy Mother. The Mother sang out,

> O Mother Divine, Thou art beyond
> The scriptural verses of Purushasuktha
> (Scriptural text which glorifies the Universal Being).
> O Mother, Thou art beyond the Brahmasutra
> (Scriptural text which describes the Absolute Brahman).
> O Mother, even transcending all the four Vedas,
> O Mother, Thou alone knowest Thee indeed.

At this point the Mother started laughing, an external expression of her inner bliss. This mysterious laughter persisted as the brahmacharins continued singing. The Mother clapped her hands like a little child and immediately raised both hands above her head. Now the laughter stopped, but her hands remained in the uplifted position for a while. The fingers of each hand displayed two different divine mudras. A beatific glow illumined her face. Bringing her hands down, the Mother again sang,

> O Mother, seeking Thee, this child will cry,
> Wandering along the shores of many seas;
> O Mother, to each and every particle of sand
> This child inquires about Thee.
> O stars, glittering in the vast blue sky,
> Did any one of you see my Mother
> Passing through this way?

The Mother sang these lines repeatedly, over and over again. The shawl which covered her head had fallen down as Gayatri tried to place it back into position. Strands of her hair fell loose around her neck and gently swirled around as her head swayed with the rhythm of the music. Tears trickled down her cheeks. Raising her hands up, the Mother went on calling, "Amma... Amma... Amma..." This went on until finally she burst into a flood of tears, but the next moment the Mother took a long, deep breath and became still. Her hands still manifested divine mudras. The brahmacharins went on singing,

> O my Mother Bhairavi, there is no shore
> Where I have not searched for Thee,
> O Mother, my darling Mother,

Bliss-embodied One,
No time exists when I have not sought for Thee,
O my Beloved Mother, for aeons and aeons
Hast Thou hid from me,
This poor child of Thine.
O Compassionate One, why dost Thou delay
To shower Thy Grace upon this child?

In the light of the burning oil lamp everyone could see the radiant
face of the Holy Mother. No sign of external consciousness was evident. Saturated with divinity, the atmosphere evoked spontaneous
meditation in the minds of all who were present, devotees and residents alike. One could easily discern that they were all singing with
their minds fully fixed on the object of their meditation. Some sang
with their minds totally focused on their Beloved Deity, shedding
tears of bliss, while others sat unmoving, deeply absorbed in profound meditation. Struggling to bring her mind down to the physical
plane of consciousness, the Holy Mother once again sang,

O Mother,
On Thy fingertips revolve hundreds,
Nay, millions of universes;
How is it justified if Thou makest me,
This poor child, also revolve
On the same fingertips of Thine?

Again the Mother was transported to her own world of infinite bliss.
She lost her control to stay in this physical plane and stood up. As she
walked towards the coconut grove in her ecstatic rapture, she allowed
herself to drown completely in the ocean of love and supreme devotion. Such was her God-intoxicated state. Spellbound, the
brahmacharins and devotees continued to glorify the Divine Mother as
they sang,

O Mother, come to me,
Stand in front of me today;
I wish to inundate Thy Holy Feet with my tears.
O Mother, the sound that rings in my heart,
The emergent tune from my heart
Is the call of loving devotion unto Thee.

O Mother, other than that,
I need nothing...

The bhajan ended with these lines. Enjoying the experience of bliss
and the fervor of pure devotion and love, everyone sat immersed in
meditation. Total silence prevailed, the silence of inner peace. This
hallowed atmosphere hung suspended in a sacred stillness as the cool,
gentle breeze floated the beckoning call of the ocean from the west.

After the arati, everyone's eyes and hearts reached out in search of
the Holy Mother. Standing at a respectful distance, they all watched
the Mother dancing in pure bliss. It felt as if the Mother was dancing all around the entire Ashram even though she was only encir-
cling that one particular spot in the coconut grove. Completely lost
to this external world in which we were standing, she reveled in her
own mystical inundation of splendor.

Swami Amirtaswarupananda, *Awaken Children*, vol. III, p. 261

Overwhelmed with Bliss

It was six o'clock in the evening. It was a beautiful sight to see the
sun setting on the western horizon into the Arabian Sea. The waves
gleefully danced, singing the ever vibrant sound OM. The Holy
Mother, accompanied by the residents and devotees, began singing
devotional songs sitting on the front verandah of the temple. Mother
slowly became more and more absorbed in the singing.

O Thou Who art meditated upon in
thousands of hearts,
Thou blazest forth forever in the minds
of those who have realized God...

As the Mother sang these lines, She became overwhelmed with bliss
and merged in a state of divine inebriation. She began crying like a
small child, now and then calling out, "Amma, Amma!" followed by
ecstatic laughter which continued for a long time. The residents and
devotees also were filled with bliss as they continued singing, drinking the nectar of the Divine Name. By this time, the Holy Mother had
gotten up from Her seat and had come to the front yard of the temple.
She began a rapturous dance punctuated with blissful laughter. Some

of the brahmacharins who were watching the scene became oblivious to the surroundings and shed tears of joy. Some others sat and got merged in meditation.

Eventually Mother's father came to the spot and caught hold of Her and made Her lie down on a mat thinking that something very serious had happened to his daughter. But the Holy Mother was still in another world, Her hands holding a mudra31 and Her face radiating like the rising sun. When She finally came down to the normal plane of consciousness, one among the devotees said, "We were concerned that Mother would have gone on and on dancing if Sugunanandan had not caught hold of Her."

Mother: "He should not have done that. It was not good. It is unbearable if someone even touches the body during such occasions. Now the whole body is burning. It is due to being touched. In the future, be attentive without letting anyone touch."
Ammachi and Swami Amritaswarupananda, *Awaken Children*, vol. 1, p. 39

FACE LIKE THE FULL MOON

Even though the evening bhajan at 6:30 p.m. was a daily routine, one never tired of singing devotional songs with Mother. She had first begun singing and composing devotional songs to God when She was very young. Her singing was an outpouring of supreme devotion and all-encompassing love, and every evening those who gathered together for bhajans would always find Her presence an elevating experience. It was easy for one's mind to readily flow toward one's Ishta Deva (beloved deity) as one's heart overflowed with Divine Love. On this particular night Her whole being radiated with spiritual glory and splendor as She sang Pakalantiyil.

Time has reached the end of the day,
But my Mother has not yet arrived.
To sit alone, this one is afraid, O my Mother.

How long must this aching heart weep helplessly?
Who is there to give company to this one
Enveloped in darkness, O my Mother?

As Mother repeated some of the lines over and over again, She soared to a high, exalted mood. Tremendous vibrations of Her singing filled the evening twilight. At last, She continued the song with tears streaming down Her cheeks...

> Do You take it as a play?
> If so, I do not understand Your viewpoint.
> Why such a fate? Is it because
> I have not uttered Your Holy Name?
>
> This one always searches with an aching heart
> For Thy Lotus Feet.
> Give me the taste of that sweet nectar
> Of devotion in my heart.

Everyone present was deeply moved upon seeing Mother cry. Hardly anyone could control his tears and some even cried aloud like Her. Spiritual bliss prevailed everywhere as everyone was totally transported to an inner realm of joy. Suddenly Mother took a long, deep breath, and the crying stopped. Her body was absolutely still. Everyone became frightened to see Her holding Her breath for such a long time. She sat in a perfect meditation posture with Her eyes half-closed. The inner bliss manifested outwardly as Her face glowed like the full moon. There was still no sign of breathing as this state continued. Some brahmacharins felt that singing might help to bring Mother down to a normal state, so they sang, beginning with a slow tempo...

> Sita Ram Sita Ram Sita Ram Bol...
> Radhe Shyam Radhe Shyam Radhe Shyam Bol...

Gradually, step by step, the cadence increased until it reached a very fast tempo. All those present sang and sang with all their hearts. As the song continued in full swing, Mother let out a blissful laugh. She raised both Her hands, which held divine mudras, and at one point She placed both hands on top of Her head. Her eyes remained closed while the laughter of ecstasy continued. This divine mood of the Holy Mother lasted for a few minutes before it slowly subsided. The residents sang the arati as one brahmacharin waved the camphor flame inside the shrine, and then the closing prayers were chanted.

The Mother continued to sit in the same place with Her eyes fixed skywards. After a while, She got up, but because She had not yet fully come out of the exalted state, Her steps faltered as She tried to walk. Assisted by two women devotees, Mother went to Her room.

Swami Amritaswarupananda, *Awaken Children*, vol. IV, p. 129

ONCE YOU TASTE IT

It was seven in the morning. The Holy Mother was sitting in the front yard of the temple where the coconut trees were growing. She was in an abstracted mood. After half an hour She got up and walked around like one who was drunk. Some times She turned around with Her eyes closed showing a particular gesture (mudra) with Her right hand. At other times, She uttered certain words as if to an unseen person still showing the mudra but at a different angle.

She roamed around for some more time fully absorbed and then all of a sudden broke into a rapturous song,

> O Mother, for the satisfaction of my life, give a drop of Thy love to my dry burning heart.
> Why O why dost Thou put burning fire as fertilizer to this scorched creeper?
>
> O Devi, chanting the Name 'Durga, Durga' my mind has forgotten all other paths.
> O my Durga, I want neither heaven nor Liberation.
> I want only pure devotion to Thee...

Hearing the song the brahmacharins who were watching from a distance slowly gathered around the Mother. As She sang, tears of bliss and devotion rolled down Her cheeks. When the song was over, in a semiconscious mood, the Mother slowly sat down and remained still for a while. Then, turning to the brahmacharins, Mother softly said, "Children, the sweetness of devotion is incomparable. Once you taste it, you will never enjoy tasting the objects of the world."

Ammachi and Swami Amritaswarupananda, *Awaken Children*, vol. I, p. 197

DRINKING MILK

As usual the sun god, the illuminer of the universe, emerged on the eastern horizon slowly sending forth brilliant rays to caress the earth and its creatures. Gazing at the beautiful rising sun, the Holy Mother was lying in the front yard of the old temple. While looking at the sun, Her mind soared to the heights of supreme bliss and, getting up in a semi-conscious mood, She walked into the shrine with faltering steps like one intoxicated. Having entered the temple, Mother started singing loudly calling out, "Amma...Amma!" now and then. After a couple of minutes, the Mother abruptly stopped singing and, placing Her head on the peetham (the seat She sat on for the Devi Bhava), started chanting 'Aum' the sacred syllable. She became totally lost to this world. Eventually She began rolling on the ground this side and that.

One hour passed like this when She suddenly got up and began dancing blissfully having placed on Her head the idol of Lord Krishna which was kept in the temple. Replacing the idol in the same spot, the Holy Mother emerged from the temple still in the same blissful mood. It was then that She noticed that the milk brought for Her by a devotee had been tipped over by the crows and spilled on the floor. The Mother sat on the floor and drank some of the milk by scooping it from the floor with Her cupped hands. Thus the Mother fulfilled the wish of the devotee who had brought the milk for Her. The next moment, the Mother joined the children who were playing games in the front yard of the temple. Now She looked exactly like a small mischievous child sporting with Her playmates.

Although seemingly contradictory, these crazy actions of the Mother were full of significance in the eyes of spiritually elevated people. Such childlike sports of the Holy Mother added visual splendor and delight to the eyes of the devotees.

Swami Amritaswarupananda, *Awaken Children*, vol. I, p. 25

AS LIGHT AS A BASKET OF FLOWERS

The evening bhajan started as usual at six-thirty. The singing reached its peak as the Holy Mother sang,

O Beautiful One, please come,
O Consort of Purandara (Lord Siva), please come,
O Auspicious One, please come...

O Giver of radiance,
Thou art the All in all of those
Who consider Thee as their dear relation...

O Mother, please remain as the spring of my inspiration...

Becoming intoxicated with God-love and, standing up, the Mother began dancing ecstatically. The brahmacharins went on singing with overflowing devotion. From the temple verandah the Mother moved towards the coconut trees in the front yard. When She reached the coconut trees She danced round and round completely lost to this world. She was showing a divine gesture (mudra) with Her right hand which was slightly raised. A beaming smile lit Her face which was clear even in the dim light. This ecstatic mood had gone on for more than half an hour and it seemed as though there would be no end to it. Some sat nearby and others at a distance watching the Mother. Some of the brahmacharins made a chain by holding hands to protect Mother from hitting the coconut trees. Eventually Sugunanandan, because of his usual fear that his daughter would leave Her body soon if this state persisted for a long time, appeared on the scene. Without asking anybody's permission, he carried Her into the hut and laid Her on a cot. Mother was totally lost to this world and Her body now seemed like a corpse. Sugunanandan later related, "The little one's body was so light in weight that it felt like I was lifting a basketful of flowers, but Her face was glowing like the rising sun."

Swami Amritaswarupananda, *Awaken Children*, vol. 1, p. 118

PERFECT DEVOTEE

That evening during the devotional singing, the Mother became intoxicated with divine love as She sang:

Aren't Thou my Mother, O aren't Thou the dear Mother who wipes away one's tears?

Aren't Thou the Mother of the fourteen worlds? O Mother,
aren't Thou the Creator of this world?

For so many days I have been calling Thee, O Supreme Energy. Won't Thou come? Won't Thou come?

Tears rolled down Her cheeks. She laughed blissfully calling,
"Amma...Amma...!" Now Her mood was that of a perfect devotee
crying for God's Vision with an overflowing heart. There were many
devotees present and all were spellbound hearing the Mother's bhajan.
Like Her presence, Her singing also gave tremendous solace to the
devotees. Some sat in contemplation and others clapped their hands,
their bodies swaying to the ecstatic music. The brahmacharins were
also totally absorbed. It seemed like a kingdom of bliss.

Swami Amritaswarupananda, *Awaken Children*, vol. I p. 127

A STRUGGLE TO STAY DOWN

It was three o'clock in the afternoon and the Holy Mother was sitting on the front verandah of the temple. Calling "Sreekumar!" the
Mother then started singing a song. Sreekumar came with the
harmonium and sat near Mother. The Mother gave certain instructions to him about the song and it's music. She Herself set the music
to it and began singing each line. In between, She told certain things
to Sreekumar about the beat of the song. She clapped Her hands according to the rhythm. Balu, Pai and Ganga came and sat near
Mother and Venu came and played the drums. Such occasions,
when Mother would compose and sing music with Her spiritual children, were really blissful moments. Unforgettable and unique were
these times.

Eventually the Holy Mother sang the song creating an overflow of
devotion, bliss and love which engulfed everyone there.

O Mother, make me mad with Thy Love!
What need have I of knowledge or reason?
Make me drunk with Thy Love's wine.

O Thou who stealest Thy devotees' hearts,
drown me deep in the Sea of Thy Love!

Intoxicated by the song, Mother got up and started moving round and round. She was in an abstracted mood. The speed of Her circling increased and in that state of total absorption, the Holy Mother now and then burst into blissful laughter. No sign of an end was to be seen. Sugunanandan, who was watching the whole scene, became very anxious about his daughter and in great consternation caught hold of Her calling "My child!" and made Her lay down on his lap. He didn't stop there. Before anybody could prevent him, he poured water on the Mother's head. Totally transported to a world unknown to those of gross intellect, the Mother burst into an uproarious laugh. It became louder and continued unabated. Half an hour passed as the laugh of uncontrollable and overflowing supreme bliss continued.

All the family members gathered around the Holy Mother. The Mother's sisters started crying and Mother Damayanti also cried calling the Divine Mother. Owing to their spiritual ignorance they thought that the Holy Mother was going to lose Her mental balance. It took a long time for the Mother to come down to the normal state. Afterwards, it seemed as though She was struggling to keep Her mind down. Her eyes went up and got fixed at the point between the eyebrows. A little over three hours later Mother regained Her external awareness. She got up from Her father Sugunanandan's lap and told him, "Father Sugunanandan, from now on don't touch my body on such occasions." Several times the brahmacharins as well as some learned people had told Sugunanandan and the other family members not to disturb the Mother during such times. But they could neither control their emotions nor could they understand the situation.

Later, the brahmacharins as instructed by the Mother Herself, would sing bhajans during that time. In those days Mother would lose Her external awareness almost every day. It would take a long while, sometimes even hours, for Her to come down. As the number of brahmacharins increased, the Holy Mother controlled Herself from getting totally absorbed. About this, She said one day, "If Mother always lets Herself get into that mood of supreme bliss, then the very purpose of taking this body will be defeated. Mother has a lot of very important work to do, including the raising of the brahmacharins." Ammachi and Swami Amritaswarupananda, *Awaken Children*, vol. 1, p. 182

VICTORY, VICTORY TO THE MOTHER

As She completed this last sentence, the Mother stood up. Her body became perfectly still. A benevolent smile formed on Her lips and Her face glowed with spiritual radiance. Both of Her hands manifested mudras; Her hair and sari danced in the sea breeze that blew from the west. She was obviously alone in a world of bliss. The devotees gazed at the Mother's face with unblinking eyes.

Balu and Pai sang a song which depicted the dancing form of Mother Kali, while Sreekumar and Venu accompanied them on harmonium and tabla.

> Victory, victory to the Mother
> Who is the Holy Consort of Lord Shiva
> And who is the Bestower of Supreme Devotion
> And Liberation.
>
> O Ocean of Compassion, who has caused
> This world of plurality to manifest,
> O Mother, please always dance
> In the heart of this humble servant
> Who remembers Thee constantly.

Some brahmacharins meditated while others joined in the singing. After twenty minutes the Holy Mother opened Her eyes and walked with staggering steps. Like one intoxicated, She moved toward the backwaters and sat there for some time. Getting up, She walked to and fro in a bliss-intoxicated mood with both Her hands on the top of Her head.

Ammachi and Swami Amirtaswarupananda, *Awaken Children*, vol. II, p. 137

PLAY THE RIGHT BEAT

The evening bhajan started at six-thirty. The Holy Mother was also present. It was raining heavily with thunder and lightning. The haunting roar of the ocean waves beating on the sand during the storm served as a constant drone from the west. The bhajan continued. The Mother in her spiritually intoxicated mood swung from side to side as she sang. The sound of the dripping rain drops provided background accompaniment for the song Amme Bhagavati Nitya Kanye Devi...

O Mother Divine, the Eternal Virgin,
I bow to Thee for Thy gracious glance.

O Maya, Mother of the Universe,
O Pure Awareness-Bliss,
O Great Goddess, I bow to Thee.

O Source of all the mantras in the four Vedas,
I bow to Thee again and again.

O Thou, the Parrot in the nest of Omkara,
I bow to Thy Holy Feet.

O Thou Who dwellest in the
Lotus face of Lord Brahma,
O Essence of the four Vedas, I bow to Thee.

All of a sudden the Mother's voice was heard above the music, "Who is that son?"

The bhajan abruptly stopped. There was utter silence. Nobody understood why the Mother asked this question. Each one thought that he had done something wrong as the Mother again asked, "Who is that who played the wrong talam (beat)? Do not overburden yourself with great sin by doing so. Missing time while singing bhajans will bring harm. If you do not play with concentration, you will miss the talam. Many celestial beings and subtle beings are listening while we sing. Each instrument has a devata (demi-god). That devata will curse if we do not play the talam correctly."

This is another example of the discipline the Mother teaches as she uses every situation to impress upon the children how they must be ever-mindful of the actions they perform, even while playing an instrument.

They continued with the bhajan:

O Goddess of the world, it is just Thy play
To create the world and save it by undoing it.

O Mind of the mind, O Dearest Mother,
I am just a mere worm in Thy play.

O Thou who art merciful to the afflicted
Who doest everything without doing anything,
I bow to Thee.

O Kali of black hue,
Destroyer of the demon Mahisha,
Sankari, whose eyes are like petals of a lotus,
I bow to Thee.

O Thou who art ever young, Destroyer of sorrow,
O Thou of Great Soul, Bhaskari, I bow to Thee.

The singing continued until quarter-past-eight when the bhajan and
the arati were concluded. The Mother remained on her seat leaning
against the wall. Her eyes were closed as the devotees and the residents prostrated to her one by one. Still in an ecstatic mood, she continued every now and then to sing some kirtans. The inner bliss in
which she reveled manifested itself outwardly as bursts of laughter.

After some time she lay down on the lap of a boy who was hardly
seven years old. She returned to her normal mood and began patting
and caressing the boy. The Mother asked him to sing. He sang
Kanna Ni Yenne...

O Krishna, have You forgotten me?
O Thou with the color of a stormy cloud,
Have you forgotten me?
Not seeing You, my suffering increases
And my heart is unable to understand anything.

The Mother seemed very absorbed in the little boy's innocent devotion and singing. There was a beautiful smile on her face. When the
boy finished the song, she asked, "Son, do you know Manasa Vacha?"

He answered, "Yes."

"Then sing," she requested.

The boy could hardly sing the first four lines. He stopped and softly told the Mother, "That's all I know."

The Mother went on singing the song celebrating the Divine, as both the devotees and the residents were gathered around her witnessing all the different moods she displayed.

> Through my mind, speech and actions,
> I remember Thee incessantly.
> Why then art Thou delaying
> To show Thy mercy to me, Beloved Mother?
>
> Years have passed
> But still my mind has no peace,
> O darling Mother, please grant me some relief.
>
> My mind sways like a boat caught in a storm,
> O Mother, give me a little peace of mind
> Lest I become a lunatic.
>
> I am tired, Mother, it is unbearable;
> I do not want such a life,
> I cannot stand Your tests,
> O Mother, I cannot endure it!
>
> I am a miserable destitute
> I have no one but You, Mother
> Please stop Your tests,
> Extend Your hand and pull me up.

Ammachi and Swami Amirtaswarupananda, *Awaken Children*, vol. III, p. 202

CHAKKA KALI

The bhajan began. The Mother was transported to a rapturous mood. She raised both her hands and called aloud, "Amme, hey...Devi, my Mother." Soaring to the highest peak of spiritual bliss, the Mother sang, Amme Bhagavati Kali Mate...

> O Mother, Supreme Goddess Kali,
> Today I will catch hold of You and devour You.

Hear what I say!
I was born under the star of death.

A child born
Under such a planetary conjunction
Devours its own mother.
So either You eat me
Or I will eat You this very day itself!

I am not going to keep quiet
Unless I know of Your choice.
Since you are black
That blackness will rub off all over my body.

When Kala, Lord of Death, comes
With rope and rod
And tries to catch me with His noose,
I will smear the black ash
From my body onto His face!

How can I, who have contained Kali within me,
Be caught in the hand of Death?
Chanting the Name, "Kali,"
I will mock at Kala!

The Holy Mother continued singing the refrain (first verse above).
The tempo reached its heights. All of a sudden the Mother got up
from her seat and began dancing blissfully and rhythmically. This
continued for some time. Then she moved toward the coconut groves
and slowly disappeared in the darkness. Everyone got up to watch her
but continued singing the same song in the same tempo a little while
longer. Nobody went near the Mother as everyone felt that it was better to leave her alone when she was in this kind of ecstatic state.

Through the darkness everyone could see the white clothes of the
Mother. She now walked like one who was in oblivion. Her steps faltered. The fear that she might hit herself against a coconut tree made
Gayatri and a few brahmacharins move toward her and keep a watchful eye on her. At one point she threw herself on the ground, which
was wet from the rain, and started rolling around. Her infinite inner

bliss manifested itself as continuous joyful laughter. Sometimes she clapped her hands and raised them skyward. The fingers of both her hands held two different divine mudras. The Mother made a noise with her tongue which sounded like the peculiar sound of satisfaction and contentment which one makes after having tasted something very delicious. She was completely lost to this world. The Mother remained in this enchanted spiritual mood for a very long time.

One would wonder if she were the same person, who sported like a small little child on the seashore and later in the game Chakka Kali, who now became so immensely intoxicated with Divine Bliss.

Slowly the Mother's body became still. She remained lying for a while longer. Gayatri went near her and made sure that she had returned to her normal mood. She then sat down near the Holy Mother. The brahmacharins also got closer and sat on either side of her. In a few minutes the Mother sat up and remained seated.

Swami Amirtaswarupananda, Awaken Children, vol. III, p. 233

HANDFUL OF SAND

Late in the evening, after the bhajan, Mother was lying down in the sand on the south side of the temple. Her head was on Gayatri's lap and Her feet rested on the lap of another woman devotee. Almost all of the brahmacharins and other Ashram residents were present. Mother was in a very playful mood. Like a child, She caught hold of Gayatri's hair and pulled. Gayatri bent her head down, but Mother kept pulling until Gayatri's head touched Mother's chest. Then She let go of the hair.

The next moment Mother closed Her eyes and with Her right hand outstretched, She went into samadhi. Everybody remained still. After a while, She came out of this mood, whirling Her right hand in circles and uttering a distinctive sound which She makes such times when She moves in and out of samadhi. Mother did not speak; neither did the brahmacharins ask any questions.

After a short while She placed Her right hand on the ground and began to dig a small hole. Suddenly She took a handful of sand, and threw it at one brahmacharin's face. As he coughed and spat, struggling to remove the sand from his mouth, Mother roared with laughter. She rolled off Gayatri's lap onto the sand, laughing uncontrollably. After a few moments, She sat up and again grabbed another handful of sand. The brahmacharins watched this, and expecting a faceful of sand, some began to move quickly away. But She did not throw any. Seeing that Mother had stopped playing, the brahmacharins who had run away now returned. But as they sat down, the sand came flying. Mother's aim was perfect. The very same brahmacharins who had run away were now showered with sand. They rushed to the water tap to wash their faces and rinse their mouths, and when they returned, Mother was in Her normal mood.

Swami Amirtaswarupananda, *Awaken Children*, vol. IV, p. 155

SIT LIKE THIS FOR MONTHS

Mother wasn't able to finish the song. Her eyes overflowed with tears. Gradually, She closed Her tear-filled eyes and sat quietly, forming a mudra with Her hand. Waves of the immeasurable power of the divine state She was in emanated from Her, awakening the hearts of those present. After awhile Her eyes opened, then closed again. It seemed as if Mother was struggling to withdraw from Her elevated state and to come back down. On an earlier occasion, Mother had gone into samadhi during bhajans and had returned to Her normal state only after several hours. At that time She had said, "If this happens, you children should sing kirtans. Otherwise, Amma could sit like this for months, or She could turn into an "avadhut[6]." Remembering that incident, the brahmacharis [monks in training] now continued to sing kirtans until Mother emerged from Her bhava. It took a long time for Her to become completely aware of Her surroundings.

Swami Jnanamritananda Puri, *Eternal Wisdom*, vol. II, p. 207 [brackets by author]

---

[6] Avadhut – one who, having merged in oneness, retains no "mask" or ego shell of compassion to serve as a vehicle for interaction with others. They experience this world and its inhabitants as an illusory dream, and, therefore, there is no suffering to relieve and no one to help. Typically, they have abandoned all social conventions and do not engage in serving or helping others to realize God.

A Movie

After supper at around 10:30 p.m., the family members wanted the Mother to watch a video movie which depicted the stories and experiences of great devotees of the Divine Mother. To fulfill their wish the Mother agreed to watch this film with them, and as She watched it, She became uncontrollably intoxicated with Divine Love. One of the stories was about a fisherman who had an innocent, pure love for the Divine Mother. He was illiterate, but he had an intense longing to see Devi [God as the Divine Mother] in flesh and blood. The Mother's mood completely changed as She watched this story. She jumped up from the seat and started dancing and singing. The sounds which She made while in that rapturous mood were varied, but they cannot be transcribed into words. In ecstatic laughter, the Mother embraced and kissed some of the girls and the elderly lady next to Her as She sat down again.

After watching the video for a little while longer, the Mother got up and went to Her room. She was still in an exalted mood as She left. It seemed that the Mother wanted to avoid seeing the movie anymore, for it might carry Her away into a totally uncontrollable state.

Swami Amritaswarupananda, *Awaken Children*, vol. IV, p. 284

A Tidal Wave of Devotion

A group of devotees who had come from the northern part of Kerala started singing verses from the Devi Mahatmyam:

O Devi, You who remove the sufferings of Your supplicants, be gracious. Be propitious, O Mother of the world. Be gracious, O Mother of the universe. Protect the universe. You are, O Devi, the ruler of all that is moving and unmoving.

You are the sole substratum of the world, because You subsist in the form of the earth. By You, who exist in the form of water, all this (universe) is gratified. O Devi of inviolable valor.

You are the power of Vishnu, and have endless valor. You are the primeval maya, which is the source of the universe; by You all this (universe) has been thrown into an illusion, O

Devi. If You become gracious, You become the cause of final emancipation in this world.

All lores are Your aspects, O Devi; so are all women in the world, endowed with various attributes. By You alone, the Mother, this world is filled. What praise can there be for You who are of the nature of primary and secondary expression regarding (objects) worthy of praise?

There was so much love and devotion in their melodious chanting of the Sanskrit slokas that some of them became very absorbed. Lost in their own world of ecstasy, they began displaying different gestures—stretching out their arms toward Amma, raising them high, joining the palms of their hands and saluting Amma. Some shed tears of love as they continued singing the chant with tremendous devotion. The devotees were thrilled at the chance to sing for Amma. As Amma sat looking at them, compassion flowed from Her eyes. Her face shone like the full moon. Amma's mere glance with the bewitching smile She wore on Her lips threw a spell of quivering enchantment over the devotees. Tears rolled down their cheeks as they soared to heights of supreme devotion while they continued to chant the hymn.

Amma sat very still on the cot. She manifested all the signs which She expresses during Devi Bhava—Her hands held in a divine mudra, a blissful smile radiating from Her face—as She gazed at the devotees who were chanting. A tidal wave of supreme devotion arose in them as their singing became more ecstatic and the entire hut vibrated to its fullness. She sat in that mood for some time, then She turned away from them but remained in an indrawn state. The chant slowly subsided. Perfect silence prevailed in the darshan hut. The devotees experienced the bliss of deep meditation. One of the devotees was in a totally intoxicated mood. With a heart filled with devotion and love, he cried and laughed at the same time as he called out "Amma... Amma" every now and then. Some of the devotees sat fixing their gaze on the Holy Mother's face. Nearly five minutes passed in this way before Amma slowly opened Her eyes chanting "Shiva...Shiva... Shiva...Shiva..." while moving Her right hand in circles, a familiar but inexplicable gesture to the devotees.

Swami Amritaswarupananda, *Awaken Children*, vol. V, p. 158

At one point Balu was describing the Mahatma's intense longing to realize God. He was depicting the excruciating pain of separation from his beloved deity through the following song, Kera vrikshannale...

> O trees and creepers,
> Have you seen my Mother?
> O glittering stars,
> Where has my Mother gone?
> O birds of the night that sing in the trees,
> Did my Mother pass this way?
> O Lady Night,
> Where can I find my Mother?
>
> I am wandering along every shore,
> crying and seeking my Mother.
> O my Beloved Mother,
> I will ask every particle of sand
> To tell me where You are.

Hearing these verses and their description of the intense yearning and agony of separation, Amma entered into a deep state of samadhi. At first She silently shed tears of bliss and then, suddenly, Amma burst into blissful laughter. After this had gone on for some time, in Her ecstasy, Amma began to roll very fast on the ground like a spinning wheel. As She rolled around, Amma continued to laugh. For some time, the brahmacharins watched in wonder and awe. But when after a few minutes Amma showed no sign of coming out of Her ecstatic mood, they began to worry. It was not the first time that they had seen Mother like this, and in the past, She Herself had instructed them to sing bhajans in order to coax Her back to the normal plane of consciousness should She remain in samadhi for more than a short while. And so, gathering in a corner of Amma's small room, the five brahmacharis began quietly to sing Nirvanashatkam (Manobuddhya).

> I am not the mind, intellect, ego or memory,
> I am not the taste of the tongue
> Or the senses of hearing, smell and sight,

I am not earth, fire, water, air or ether.
I am Pure Bliss Consciousness.
I am Shiva.

I am not right or wrong actions,
Nor am I pleasure or pain.
I am not the mantra or any sacred places,
The Vedas or the sacrifice.
I am not the act of eating, the eater or the food.
I am Pure Bliss Consciousness.
I am Shiva.

I have no birth or death,
Nor have I any fear.
I don't hold any caste distinction.
I have not father or mother
Associates or friends.
I have no Guru
And I have no disciple.
I am Pure Bliss Consciousness.
I am Shiva.

I have no form
Or movements of the mind.
I am the all-pervasive.
I exist everywhere,
Yet I am beyond the senses.
I am not salvation
Or anything that may be known.
I am Pure Bliss Consciousness.
I am Shiva.

In Her God-intoxicated state, Amma continued to roll and laugh for ten or fifteen minutes. Finally She got up from the floor and began moving around the room as if drunk. Amma stumbled about with faltering steps, laughing blissfully all the while. Her fingers were held in identical divine mudras, and Her face glowed, emitting a penetrating radiance. Several times Amma's head or body came close to hitting the walls or banging against the floor, but the brahmacharins were very watchful and protected Her from any possible harm. For some time, Amma remained in one spot and gently swayed from side to side, reveling in Her own world, a world to which no one else had access. Eventually Amma lay down on the floor and remained still. The brahmacharins continued to sing until Amma had finally descended from Her exalted state.

Swami Amritaswarupananda, *Awaken Children*, vol. VI, p. 201

THE BLISS-INTOXICATED MOTHER

There were clouds in the sky. It looked as if it was about to rain. The sound of the ocean waves grew louder and a strong, cool wind came blowing through the air. Mother looked up at the sky and at once became deeply absorbed in a spiritual mood. By now the sun was completely covered by dark rain clouds. Though it was only eleven-thirty in the morning, it looked as if night was approaching. Soon it began to drizzle. Bri. Gayatri came down from Mother's room with an umbrella and held it over Mother's head. The residents didn't move but continued to sit in the rain next to Mother. Within a few seconds the rain was pouring down. But Mother continued to sit in the same spot with Her gaze still directed towards the sky.

A few minutes later Mother got up and walked into the rain, and She began to play like a child. She jumped about and danced in circles, now and then pausing in the pouring rain to look up at the sky. She would stand with Her arms outstretched, Her open palms facing up toward the sky as if She was trying to catch the rain drops in Her hands. All the residents were standing a few yards away, watching this beautiful scene.

Mother was by now completely drenched. Gayatri stood helplessly by Her side with the folded umbrella in her hands. Suddenly, Mother joined Her palms together above Her head, and began to turn around in a circle. And as She did so, She recited the following verse.

Anandam Saccitanandam
Anandam Paramanandam
Anandam Saccitanandam
Anandam Brahmanandam

The Bliss of Pure Existence/Consciousness
The Bliss of Supreme Bliss
The Bliss of Pure Existence/Consciousness
The Bliss of Absolute and Undivided Bliss

Long after the song had come to an end, Mother continued to circle round and round. Her palms were still joined above Her head and Her eyes were closed. There was no sign of Her having any body consciousness at all. She was transported to another world. Her face was radiant and enchanting. There was a beautiful, divine smile on Her lips, and as She continued Her dance, rain water dripped through Her black, cascading hair and streamed down Her cheeks.

Nobody knew what to do. Somebody suggested that they carry Her inside. But Br. Nealu thought that they shouldn't touch Mother as long as She was in that state of bliss. While they were discussing among themselves what to do, Mother slowly stopped Her dance and lay down on the ground, which by now had become a pool of muddy water. And as She lay in the rain without moving, the spiritual glow continued to radiate from Her face.

The rain continued to pour as heavily as before and the residents grew increasingly anxious. Bri. Gayatri who was sitting next to Mother on the soaking wet ground, trying to shield Her with the umbrella, insisted that they should carry Mother inside. Finally everyone agreed and did as she directed.

As soon as Mother had been brought into Her room, Gayatri requested everyone to leave so that she could remove Mother's wet clothes. Everybody left immediately and the door was closed. Mother remained in the state of samadhi for a long time.

What can one say about such a mysterious personality, who at one moment is the great Master and the next an innocent child, and who then again, a few seconds later, slips into the highest state of samadhi?
Swami Amritaswarupananda, *Awaken Children*, vol. VII, p. 188

This Is That

The song reached a very high tempo. At this point Mother got up from the place where She had been sitting with the children and went over to the women who were dancing. She looked very excited and at the same time divinely intoxicated as She joined in the dance. There was an innocent expression on Her face which made Her look like a divine child among the dancing women. The women were overjoyed to have Mother dancing in their midst.

At one stage of the dance, two ladies facing each other made a pair and clapped their open palms together. Mother who was transported to another world was still dancing but in Her own blissful way. Her eyes were closed and both hands were held in divine mudras. After dancing in circles with the ladies for some time, Mother moved toward the center of the dance where She continued to dance blissfully, while the devotees were singing a song, glorifying the Goddess Parvati.

After some time Mother stopped dancing and came to a standstill. Her external form and Her countenance were radiating with a divine glow. She looked exactly as She did during Devi Bhava. It was evident that She was still absorbed in Her divine mood. The devotees continued to dance and to sing, one song after another, until Mother finally sat down on the ground, still in that indrawn state.

The devotees had a strong feeling that Mother was in the bhava of the Goddess Parvati. Who knows? Perhaps She was revealing that mood for the benefit of the devotees. Nothing is impossible for a soul who is one with the Supreme Brahman. Such a person can manifest any aspect of the Divine at any time he wants.

When Mother finally returned to Her normal self, one of the devotees asked Her, "Amma, we strongly felt that You were in the divine mood of Goddess Parvati?"

Mother pointed first at Herself and then upward, as She replied, "This is That." After a pause She continued, "Whether or not it is manifested, this is That. Don't mistake this for the body. The body is only a cover. There is infinity beyond the cover."

The incomprehensible expression on Mother's face and the words that She uttered seemed to be coming directly from the highest plane of consciousness. If one penetrated a little, it was not difficult to discern that Mother, though not directly, was saying that She was in the divine mood of the Goddess Parvati. The depth of such a declaration was so profound and piercing that everyone was deeply touched in the innermost recesses of their hearts.

Swami Amritaswarupananda, *Awaken Children*, vol. VII, p. 200

Experiences of Devotees

A Vision of Mother as Parashakti

When the song had come to an end, a woman who was in the middle of receiving Mother's darshan, suddenly got up and began to dance and sing while she chanted the mantra, "Aum Parashaktyai Namah." The woman raised her arms above her head and joined her palms together. Her eyes were closed and tears were streaming down her cheeks. She looked very blissful. She had the serenity and joy of one who is totally absorbed in meditation.

In her state of bliss the woman exclaimed, "Blessed indeed am I today! By touching Your holy feet I have become blessed and purified. Today, I have seen Parashakti.2 O Mother, please don't leave me!"

Some devotees tried to carry her out of the room. But Mother interrupted and said, "No, no, it's alright! She's in bliss. Don't touch her. Let her dance and sing." Having received Mother's instructions, the devotees gave up the idea of carrying the woman away, and she continued to dance and sing for some time, in the same blissful mood.

Later, the woman talked about her experience: "As I was waiting in front of Mother, She looked at me and smiled so lovingly. That smile was like a blissful, electric shock to me and all my hairs stood on end. I felt as if I was losing all my body consciousness, and I fell in full prostration in front of Mother. I called out and prayed, 'O Mother, great Enchantress, protect me! O Mother, protect me! O Parvati, Lord Shiva's holy consort, give me refuge!' With infinite love and affection, Mother took hold of me, drew me toward Her and placed my head on Her lap. She then lifted my head from Her lap and applied sandal paste between my eye brows. This divine touch was another supremely blissful experience. My eyes were opened wide. It was like an outer space experience. I was completely immersed in a divine feeling, its presence so full and tangible, I felt as if I were floating in the air, floating in a feeling of perfect fullness. But what I beheld in front of my eyes was something unbelievable. It was not a dream or an illusion–it was as real and as clear as I am seeing you now."

The woman was very excited. She couldn't speak any more, as her words choked in her throat. Her eyes filled with tears and she seemed ecstatic. The listener who was anxious to hear the last part of her narration said to her, "Kindly tell me about the vision you had. What did you see?"

The lady somehow managed to control her emotions and said, "I saw the beautiful and enchanting form of Devi right in front of my eyes, in all Her splendor and glory, sitting in a lotus posture with all Her weapons. Words cannot begin to describe the wonderful experience I had. My heart was intoxicated with bliss. There was only bliss, bliss, bliss–I was drowning in supreme bliss." Even as she was talking about the experience the lady sounded very blissful.

Swami Amritaswarupananda, *Awaken Children*, vol. VII, p. 188

A DEVOTEE'S EXPERIENCE OF KALI

A devotee who had a wonderful vision the night before during Devi Bhava was sharing it with one of the residents. He was very excited and wanted some clarification about the vision. He related what had taken place. While the residents were immersed in singing bhajans, his mind was overflowing with love and devotion for the Mother. They sang a song about the Mother...Entinanamme Hara...

O Mother, Why do You stand
Keeping Your Foot on Lord Shiva?
Also what have You relished
For Your tongue to stick out?

O All-Knowing One, You always walk around
Like an ordinary girl who knows nothing;
But I know within me that this is how You are,
O Omniscent One.

Though fierce, how pleasant and compassionate
Is Your countenance, O Mother.
My longing to sleep on Your lap
Is becoming more and more intense.

O Kali, the Enchantress,
People say that You walk around intoxicated,
Having fully drunk.
O Eternal Truth, Who knows
What You drink is the Nectar of Immortality?

By placing Your Foot on Your Father's chest,
O Mother, You show us that Your Holy Feet
Can only be attained through the quality of Sattva,
By filling the mind with sattvic qualities.
O Mother, kindly bestow that quality
Upon this humble devotee as well.

His eyes were fixed on the Mother's face. All of a sudden every-thing disappeared from his sight. In a whirlpool everything seemed to dematerialize while his eyes were wide open. The temple, the people and the surroundings vanished from his sight. No singing reached his ears. The entire universe with its duality and diverse na-ture disappeared. He lost his own individuality, and even the Mother's form vanished from his sight. Though he wanted to call or shout aloud, he could not move or speak. He felt as if he were mov-ing out of his body. He experienced that he was different from his body. Then he beheld the entire universe flooded with effulgence. His eyes could not stand the light.

Slowly the light solidified into a form. While he was experiencing great difficulty in seeing, the effulgence evolved into the fierce yet enchanting form of Mother Kali dancing on the chest of Lord Shiva. There was the Great Mother's infinite spiritual glory and splendor, Her protruding tongue, big red bulging eyes, and the divine weapons which She held in Her numerous hands. Awesome as She was, the devotee was so relaxed and blissful that all the fears he had before dissolved. He expressed it this way: "Her form was such that even Lord Shiva would be afraid to go near Her, but the compassion, love and spiritual bliss which I experienced were like ambrosia, so soothing to the heart that they removed my fear and delusion."

Gradually everything returned to normal, and the devotee was thrown back into the realm of time and space. Coming back to his normal consciousness, the devotee fainted and fell backwards from his sitting position. Some other devotees who attended to him found him perspiring profusely and breathing irregularly. After taking a few gasps of air, he remained breathless for a while. As time passed people became worried, not knowing what was happening to him.

Mother, who had been watching the whole scene with a mischievous smile on Her face, sent a rose that She took from the garland She was wearing with instructions that it be held close to his nose. As soon as the rose was placed near him, he began to breathe normally. Then he opened his eyes and sat upright. The expression on his face revealed much serenity and bliss. As if returned from another world, the devotee looked around to re-orient himself. Finally, he kept his gaze on the Mother's countenance. A special, sweet smile of inexpressible joy lit his face as he sat in deep meditation throughout the night until the Devi Bhava Darshan was over.

The next morning he was still full of bliss and peace. He confessed, "I am unable to control the spiritual bliss I am experiencing which comes from deep within. It is a rare experience that Amma has bestowed upon me." The brahmacharin to whom this experience was being told felt envious of this middle-aged man who had been given the rare blessing to behold the vision of Mother Kali.

Later in the darshan hut the devotee once again saw the Holy Mother while She was giving darshan to people. He begged the Mother, "Amma, I have no doubt that you are none other than Mother Kali. It is also very clear to me that it was you who appeared as Kali in front of me. Who else could give me the darshan of Kali other than you? But, Amma, maybe it is my ignorance, but still I have the desire to hear from your own lips, 'I am Kali. It is I who gave you the darshan.' As my Guru and Ishta Devata, you must tell me that. Please, Amma, please..."

The Mother kept looking at him. There was an expression of tremendous motherly love and compassion on Her face. A few moments passed as the Mother kept quiet, yet not turning Her face away from this devotee. He began sobbing like a little child. He covered his face with both hands and fell on the Mother's lap. With great love the Mother rubbed his back and tried to console him, saying, "Son... son... don't cry, don't cry." But he couldn't help crying. Then She lovingly put him on Her shoulder and whispered something into his ear. As soon as She did this, he burst into a sudden stream of blissful laughter. He jumped up and started dancing. Laughing and crying at the same time with tears of joy rolling down his cheeks, he shouted, "Kali! Kali! Mahakali... Kali has come as my Guru and Ishta Devata. Kali! Kali! Kali..." He kept on repeating this until the Mother finally laid Her right palm on his chest to calm him down, and he returned to a normal state.

Later he related that this blissful mood lasted for about two weeks. He revealed that indeed the Holy Mother had whispered in his ears that She was the one who had given him the darshan and that She was Kali. That was the reason for his rapturous joy.

Swami Amritaswarupananda, *Awaken Children*, vol. IV, p. 258

YOUNG MAN FROM RISHIKESH

Soon after the morning meditation one of the brahmacharins noticed a young man sitting in front of the temple. He had a long beard and long hair, and there was a calm, quiet manner about him. The brahmacharin was very impressed by the young man's meditative posture and serene look. After the usual breakfast of rice gruel, served to residents and visitors alike, the brahmacharin once again came to the temple verandah to see if the young man had stirred from his meditation, but found him still deeply absorbed. Half an hour passed, and the young man was still sitting on the verandah, but his eyes were open now. The brahmacharin asked him, "Have you had your breakfast? If not, please come and have some." Very politely he answered, "No, I have not, but I do not want to eat before I see Amma."

Sitting down next to him, the brahmacharin inquired, "Where do you come from and how did you come to know about Amma?"

The young man revealed that he was from Rishikesh and proceeded to share his experience of how he came to know about the Mother. "I am also a sadhak. By God's grace I have been on the spiritual path for the last fifteen years. I live in an ashram in Rishikesh with the Ganges River only a few yards away. Every day I spend some time on the banks of the river, chanting my mantra and meditating.

"Of course, this holy river is most conducive for meditation, but recently I began to have problems in concentration due to some mental agitation. Two weeks ago while trying to meditate, I heard someone calling my name, not only once, but several times. I did not open my eyes, thinking it was only my imagination. So I continued to sit with my eyes closed and tried to concentate on the flowing sound of the Ganges. Again came the voice calling me. It was a female voice, calling me again and again. The sound was so clear that I had no doubt that someone was calling me, so I opened my eyes. I looked all around, and as I was doing this, the voice came again, 'Here, look here.' The voice seemed as if it was coming from the Ganges Herself. I sat gazing at the water and as I held my gaze, a form slowly began to take shape on the waters.

"This form became clearer and clearer, revealing itself as a woman in pure white clothes. Around Her stood many saintly-looking people who clearly showed great reverence and devotion to Her. Rubbing my eyes, I looked again and again. It was not a dream. It was a reality. My eyes were wide open. I could see this woman and all those who were standing around Her, but I could recognize none of them. A divine aura surrounded Her, and I could not take my eyes off Her.

"Radiating peace and bliss, She smiled graciously at me. Slowly I became totally unaware of the external world. The saintly-looking people who were around Her also disappeared. All that existed was the lady in white and myself. Time and space did not exist. I was all alone in Her presence. Gradually She grew bigger and bigger. She became as big as the universe, and there was nothing but Her. A strong effulgence emanated from Her whole being, and I was totally enveloped in that light. Then all of a sudden, the form disappeared and there was only pure light filling the entire universe. And then, in a split-second of a moment the light suddenly became a pin-point. That is all I could remember. I was aroused to normal awareness hearing a constant ringing in my ears. It was the same voice, 'Come to Me. Come to Me. Come to Me.'

"Gradually regaining my ordinary consciousness, I looked around. I was stunned to see that it was already dark. I looked at my watch which registered 8:30 p.m. Since I had begun sitting for meditation that afternoon at around five o'clock, this meant that nearly three and a half hours had passed. The flowing sound of the Ganges filled the air. Everything else was silent.

"I returned to the ashram. The residents wanted to know where I had been all that time since it was not my normal routine to spend such long hours outside of the ashram. My daily visit to the Ganges was usually around an hour, never more than an hour and a quarter. From the look on my face and my sudden indrawn manner, the residents suspected that something had happened to me. But I kept quiet. I did not feel like talking. The experience was so overwhelming and full. I could not sleep that night. I was haunted by the vision of that form which had appeared in front of me, and my heart and soul were totally immersed in it.

"That day marked a great transformation in my life. The next morning found me a completely changed person. The fellow ashram residents noticed this change in me and were very inquisitive, asking questions of me constantly. But my thoughts always reveled in that enchanting form of the lady whom I saw in the vision, and my heart continued to overflow with the bliss of that experience. It is not that I wanted to avoid the others, but I remained unable to speak.

"Finally the news of my behavior reached the ears of one swami who also lived in the ashram. He was a sadhak himself and a good soul. Summoning me, he lovingly inquired about the reason for the change in me, and for some reason, I felt that I wanted to disclose everything about the experience to him. I related it all to him, and I also told him that my mind was now completely absorbed in the vision of that form. I asked whether he knew anything about this lady in white. I could easily give him a description of Her since the vision was so clear. He listened to me carefully and told me that he would try to discover who She was.

"Days went by and my longing became more and more intense. I was like one gone mad. I was unable to sleep and I gave up eating. After a few days, the swami called me to see him again. He had a big smile on his face, and without any introductory remarks, he pulled out a picture from his pocket and asked if this was the lady whom I had seen. I jumped up and danced with joy because it was a picture of Her! He gave it to me and told me who She was and where Her ashram was located. He also revealed that while he had listened to me relate my experience to him, he had felt tremendous inner peace and a strong feeling that this must be a Great Soul. This caused him to immediately begin inquiring about Her, and finally he met another swami living in Rishikesh who was from Kerala. From this swami he learned about Amma."

The young man showed the picture to the brahmacharin. Full of emotion and his eyes swelling with tears, he asked, "Will I be able to see Amma today?"

The brahmacharin assured him that he would certainly be able to see the Mother, telling him that She is always available for Her children. Again he invited the young man to have some food.

He replied, "My brother, I have not been eating for many days now. I do not feel like eating. I am not hungry. Anyhow, let me see Amma first. If She asks me to eat I will do so. Until then, please do not insist that I take any food."

The brahmacharin was about to leave when he saw the Mother coming down the stairs. "Here comes Amma," he said in a soft voice.

The young man jumped up and looked around. Just as a hornbill bird waiting for water runs to catch falling raindrops, he ran toward the Mother and fell into full prostration at Her Feet. The Mother lovingly lifted him up, and holding his hands, She brought him back to the verandah of the temple. He sobbed like a little child, while She expressed tremendous love and compassion to him by patting

his back and rubbing his chest. Wiping his tears, She laid his head
on Her shoulder and consoled him, "My son, why do you cry now?
You have come to your Mother, haven't you? Son, don't cry.
Mother is here for you."

Swami Amritaswarupananda, Awaken Children, vol. IV, p. 189

TEARS OF INNER JOY

The Mother walked toward Her hut followed by Gayatri. At five,
the bhajan before Bhava Darshan began. The Holy Mother sang,

> The sound OM is ringing everywhere
> As an echo in every atom.
> With a peaceful mind,
> Let us chant "Om Sakti."
>
> O Noble One who is adored by the Universe,
> We come to know Thee well
> When this Universe is understood to be worthless
> Which so far was felt as great...

Sreekumar played the harmonium and Venu the drums. Balu and the
other brahmacharins and devotees sang along with the Holy Mother.
The Mother's songs were poignant with God-love, filling the atmosphere with waves of supreme devotion which penetrated the hearts of
the brahmacharins and devotees. All were led into a meditative mood.
It could be seen that some were silently shedding tears of inner joy.

Swami Amritaswarupananda, Awaken Children, vol. I, p. 102

EVERYONE SANG FORGETTING THEMSELVES

The bhajan began as usual at six-thirty. The Mother was playing the
ganjira (a small hand drum with only one head). In a few minutes she
put it down and picked up the cymbals and began playing. It seemed
that the Mother was struggling to keep her mind down. Now she also
put the cymbals down and sang, creating waves of unconditional bliss
which radiated all around with Manase Nin Svantamayi...

> Remember, O mind, this supreme truth:
> Nobody is your own!

Because of doing meaningless actions,
You are wandering in the ocean of this world.

Even though people honor you,
Calling you, "Lord, Lord,"
It will be for a short time only.

Your body, which has been honored for so long,
Must be cast off when life departs.

For which sweetheart have you been struggling
All this time, not even caring for your life?

Even she will be frightened by your dead body
And will not accompany you.

Trapped in the subtle snare of Maya as you are,
Do not forget the Sacred Name
Of the Divine Mother.

The Lord will attract devotion-soaked souls
Like a magnet attracts iron.

Position, prestige and wealth are impermanent;
The only Reality is the Universal Mother.

Renouncing all desires,
Let us dance in that bliss
Singing the Name of Mother Kali!

Singing with the Mother, especially in the evenings, is a joyous experience which opens the heart to a much more elevated plane of devotion. Sitting on the powerful spiritual wings of the Mother, the devotees and residents fly high every evening at bhajans, drinking in the nectarous bliss of Supreme Devotion. Each moment is an experience, exposing the heart to another spiritual treasure chest. Today also it happened. Everyone sang forgetting themselves.

Swami Amritaswarupananda, *Awaken Children*, vol. III, p. 219

Everyone sang, forgetting themselves.

THE SEQUEL TO FINDING GOD'S LOVE

Finding God's Love is a how-to book detailing the theory and practice of devotion to God. If this book has inspired you to take up the path of love and devotion, the author recommends the sequel, *Soft Moon Shining*, also written by him. *Soft Moon Shining* is poetry that flows with love for the Divine like a river of honey. Art, in this case poetry, is well suited for communicating feeling as opposed to academia. With an understanding of the path and the techniques in hand, *Soft Moon Shining* will kindle the feeling or joy of love for God. This helps the practitioner to become oriented in understanding the direction to take. More importantly, it helps one to understand the *feeling* that one is to cultivate. By analogy, *Finding God's Love* is like reading a book that tells us how to make ice cream complete with varying recipes. *Soft Moon Shining* is an actual taste of the ice cream. *Soft Moon Shining* can be purchased directly from Devi Press online at www.devipress.com or by telephone toll free 866-531-5967 or ordered from any book store. There is more information about *Soft Moon Shining* - including some sample poems - at the end of this book. Eight poems from *Soft Moon Shining* are included in the text of this book.

Bibliography

The author wishes to thank the following for quotations that
appeared in this book:

Quotations from the following used with permission of MA Center
© Copyright MA Center 1989 through 1998

Awaken Children, volumes 1 through 9
by Swami Amritaswarupananda
Mata Amritanandamayi Center
P.O. Box 613
San Ramon, CA 94583
www.ammachi.org

Quotations from the following used with permission of MA Center
© Copyright MA Center 1997 and 1999

Eternal Wisdom
Parts 1 and 2
by Swami Jnanamritananda
Mata Amritanandamayi Center
P.O. Box 613
San Ramon, CA 94583
www.ammachi.org

Gospel of Ramakrishna
by M
Ramakrishna-Vivekananda Center
17 East 94th Street
New York, NY 10128

Mother of the Universe
By Lex Hixon
Theosophical Publishing House
P.O. Box 270
Wheaton, IL 60189

Drunk on the Wine of the Beloved
Shambala Publications
Horticultural Hall
300 Massachusetts Ave.
Boston, MA 02115

Index

Other Books by the Author

The Mystic Christ
Devi Press
P.O. Box 5081
Norman, OK 73071
www.devipress.com

The Mystic Christ is an ancient tale of mystic union, salvation, and enlightenment. It is the careful uncovering of a lost treasure of immeasurable value, long buried in the suffocating darkness of conventional orthodoxy on one side, and blind fundamentalist extremism on the other. From the viewpoint of the world's mystical religious traditions, the brilliant light of the Master's way is revealed as a penetrating radical non-duality unifying all people and all of life. His path to this all-embracing unity is the spiritual practice of selfless love. Love God intensely, love our neighbor as our own Self, bless those that curse us, and pray for those that mistreat us. The central problem with our world today is that love has been lost, becoming nothing more than a word in the dictionary and, yet, love is the essential compelling message given to us by Jesus 2,000 years ago.

The Mystic Christ is also the story of the ego, the personification of ignorance, and how it has distorted and subverted the sublime sayings of the Master, twisting reality into unreality and light into darkness. The ego is the Antichrist in this ancient drama that has gripped every culture for all time in its talons of self-centered perception. The ego is anti-love.

Adam and Eve were not the first people, the original nature of man is good, scripture is not infallible, Jesus is one of the ways, all religions are paths to God, reincarnation is our future, the resurrection is a personal spiritual awakening, and no one is damned to hell for all eternity. And it's all in the Bible! These issues are carefully and lovingly revealed in the life and sayings of Jesus.

The Mystic Christ is at once profoundly fascinating, deeply historic and electric with the vibration of the mystical experience.

"*The Mystic Christ* is the greatest literary work of Mystic Christianity that I have read to date. Even though it is written in a clear, concise and elegant manner, it is still a book best consumed in small portions as the uncomplicated verbiage hides deceptively weighty truths.

"I can ask no more of a book than to change the way I perceive or experience life. *The Mystic Christ* has done both. To call it a book seems to slight the work, it would be best described as a mystical literary experience.

"What other book sums up the purpose of life in three words of one sentence (page 67)? This book is a sword that neatly slashes the Gordian Knot of the Neo-Pharisee. It is the fire in which the dross of Conventional Fundamentalist Orthodox Christianity should be purified.

"I am not usually so wordy, but this book kindled my soul. Without preaching, Ethan Walker gives a multitude of lessons on love, wisdom and compassion. He proves that religion need not be complicated, and that when distilled is a simple loving message.

"Ethan Walker quotes from Krishna, Buddha, Ammachi, Mohammed, and of course Jesus. From an eclectic mix of sources he shows that the message of love is timeless, and that the Orthodox Church does not own the only toll road to Heaven.

"I can honestly find no fault with the material, and this is not because I agreed with everything the author said. Reading this book forced upon me a personal and spiritual change. And to quote from the book, "Personal spiritual change is painfully difficult. Spiritual change leaves us empty and naked." In my reading I was, at first troubled, then I studied, prayed, checked sources, and was amazed. For the seeker of truth or for anyone who feels that salvation is more than mouthing the words "I believe in Jesus" this book is both startling and calming. While it is true that I was brought to an awareness in which I felt empty and naked, I was also brought to a place where I felt God lifted my eyes from the mud of the path I was crawling along and has begun teaching me to walk.

"While I have never met Ethan Walker III, I think he has created an amazing work that needs to be placed in as many hands as possible. I do not just recommend that you read this book, I beg you to. Within the pages of *The Mystic Christ* lies the truest and greatest 'Road map to peace,' be it in the mid-east, your neighborhood, or the world." Jeff L.

"Walker is an excellent author that has bridged the gap between Eastern mysticism and Western monasticism. In a practical how-to manner, he makes the application of meditation methods developed by Western monks adapting Eastern mysticism as found in Hinduism and Buddhism to Western religious practice. A great book." *Bruce W.*

"This book is a love letter to mankind. Having studied the Gnostic writings and teachings for a number of years, this book sheds more light on these teachings. I found the book to be extremely clear in its wording and explanations, which is what is needed for those who are just beginning with the mystical path it outlines. It delineates the differences between true spirituality and dogmatic religion with excellent examples that help those who may still be unsure to see that there is nothing to fear by questioning their religious beliefs. Although I am not a Christian, I have no problem with the references to Jesus, for I feel that he was a great teacher who was far closer to my own beliefs than to the false and dark doctrines which arose in his name. His was the path of love, and that is the basis of all true religion, no matter what it might be called. Many blessings to Ethan Walker III for having the courage and wisdom to write *The Mystic Christ* at this time when the world so needs spiritual inspiration and comfort." *Linda S.*

"I had some very interesting experiences. The main experience I continued to have all the way to the end of the book was I had to stop reading and mediate on the what I just read because the reading would challenge most of my beliefs about GOD. Some times I would think about what the author wrote for weeks and even months later. I had a few experiences where I just felt that the words in the book were truth. I know that is not a very detailed explanation of my experiences, but I feel if I try to write too many words about that I would do my experiences injustice. I would share with friends what I read in the book and discuss it with them. I have had some deep discussions about my spiritual beliefs and other people's spiritual beliefs. I just want to thank the author for the inspirational words. He sparked the spirit within me. I have recommended this book to several friends." *Robert R.*

"I was amazed at Mr. Walker's insight into the true meanings of Christ's messages. I ordered 2 more books to give to friends. I have been studying all the Eastern wisdom traditions and Christianity now for a number of years and I always felt they tied in with each other. I will be reading it over and over and over." *Jerry M.*

Soft Moon Shining
Devi Press
P.O. Box 5081
Norman, OK 73071
www.devipress.com

Eight poems from *Soft Moon Shining* have been reprinted in *Finding God's Love*. *Soft Moon Shining* is an invitation to step into the heart of the Divine Mother. Her perpetual dance of cosmic bliss plays out through the eons as the creation and dissolution of worlds within worlds. Yet God, in the feminine form of the Mother - as the Absolute made Immanent - is ready to shower Her love and affection on any who care to turn their gaze toward Her fiery heart. Included are 54 illustrations.

This work of poetry is both profound and beautiful in its ability to arrest the reader's conventional mind, plunging the soul into the cauldron of divine intoxication and immortal bliss. Each poem is a meditation on the Mother of the universe. Feel Her love and Her compassion as the Divine Mother hugs each reader in an embrace of timeless love.

Dance with God in the form of the Mother! Revel in the call of the infinite! Swoon with joy as the heart opens wide to the roaring river of Mother love. *Soft Moon Shining* continues in the tradition of those great poets and lovers of God, Ramprasad, Hafiz, and Rumi.

"Get ready to weep with joy! This book is a pure-light can opener for the heart." *William D.*

"Each poem is a profound meditation. This book is best read every day. It's overflowing with love and wisdom." *Margaret D.*

SAMPLE POEMS FROM "SOFT MOON SHINING"

SOFT MOON SHINING

> My beloved Divine Mother
> Dance with me
>   under the soft moon shining
>   in the wide open fields
>   far beyond the toil and trouble
>   of my busy mind
>
> Dance with me
>   before the night grows old
>   while the winds of love
>   still bow the grasses
>   and the coyotes cry for you
>   to step their way
>
> Dance with me my beloved
>   while the Mystery's Edge
>   still flirts in the shadow
>   of your radiant light

THE BOOK

> Mother Kali
> Place your seal on this book of mortal existence
>   now emptied of words
>   from crying to you
>
> I have given this book to you
>   to do with as you wish

as there is no one left
   who wants to write in it

Having tasted your Divine Love
   what else can be of any importance?

I am your laughing schoolboy
   playing hooky from the ceaseless pounding
     of facts and names

And I am running headlong to swim in your river of immortal
bliss
   carelessly flinging these clothes
     of concerns and considerations to the ground as I go

Hugging Arms

My beautiful Divine Mother
This universe is your body
   alive and blushing
     with cosmic streams
       and rivers of love

I bow to the rocks
   ancient siblings of boundless love

I bow to the sun and the sailing planets
   who whistle songs of love
     to one another
       from deep within the inner spheres

And I bow to every atom
   eternally in love with every other atom
     all of them whirling dervishes
       ecstatic in their dance
         of joyous coexistence

My heart melts at the sight
   of this endless love feast

And I deeply regret
   that my hugging arms
      are so few and so short

DRAW ANOTHER CUP OF JOY

Compassionate Mother
   who's grace is beyond eternity

My friends and I will draw another cup of joy
   from the wellspring
      of your radiant heart

And raise it to our lips with a shout
   Victory to the Mother!
      Victory to the Mother of all beings!

And when this tavern of divine revelry
   closes in the morning's wee hours

We will all walk home arm in arm
   with faltering steps
   to our conventional minds
      staggering with the intoxication of love
      and waking the neighbors
         shouting like bugle blowers

Victory to the Mother!
   Victory to the Mother of the universe!

DEVI PRESS

PO Box 5081, Norman OK 73070

405-447-0364 • fx 405-360-5277
www.devipress.com

Individuals: We encourage you to ask for Devi Press books at your local bookstore. If you are unable to obtain a Devi Press book from your retailer, you may call or email us or use the form below to order via fax or postal service. Mastercard and Visa accepted. Oklahoma residents please add 8.375% sales tax.

Please make checks payable to DEVI PRESS.

Qty	Title	Amount
_____	The Mystic Christ ($14.95)	_____
_____	Soft Moon Shining ($14.95)	_____
_____	Finding God's Love ($13.95)	_____

Unless otherwise specified books are shipped via US Mail ($3.00 for the first book plus $.50 for each add'l book)

Subtotal _____

Sales Tax _____
OK - 8.375%

Shipping _____

TOTAL _____

Date_____

Name_____

Address_____

City/State_____Zip_____

Phone_____

Credit Card #_____Exp._____

Signature_____